W9-BVC-609

RAILROADS

Bridging the Continents

by LOIS WARBURTON

The ENCYCLOPEDIA of

D·I·S·C·O·V·E·R·Y
and INVENTION

P.O. Box 289011 SAN DIEGO, CA 92198-0011

These and other books are included in the Encyclopedia of
Discovery and Invention series:

Airplanes: The Lure of Flight

Atoms: Building Blocks of Matter

Clocks: Chronicling Time

Computers: Mechanical Minds

Genetics: Nature's Blueprints

Germs: Mysterious Microoganisms

Gravity: The Universal Force

Lasers: Humanity's Magic Light

Movies: The World on Film

Photography: Preserving the Past

Plate Tectonics: Earth's Shifting Crust

Printing Press: Ideas into Type

Radar: The Silent Detector

Railroads: Bridging the Continents

Telescopes: Searching the Heavens

Television: Electronic Pictures

To Vicki Ann Marshak

Number One Daughter

Number One Railroad Engineer

Copyright 1991 by Lucent Books, Inc., P.O. Box 289011, San
Diego, California, 92198-0011

Library of Congress Cataloging-in-Publication Data

Warburton, Lois, 1938–
    Railroads: bridging the continents / by Lois Warburton.
      p. cm. — (The Encyclopedia of discovery and invention)
    Includes bibliographical references and index.
    Summary: Discusses the history, development, and technology of the steam
engine and railroads; examines the decline of rail transport in the United States;
and describes the growth of railroads in Europe and Japan, focusing on high-speed
trains and magnetic levitation.
    ISBN 1-56006-216-9
    1. Railroads—Juvenile literature. [1. Railroads.] I. Title. II. Series.
TF148.W37 1991
385—dc20   91-23857

Contents

■■

Foreword

The belief in progress has been one of the dominant forces in Western Civilization from the Scientific Revolution of the seventeenth century to the present. Embodied in the idea of progress is the conviction that each generation will be better off than the one that preceded it. Eventually, all peoples will benefit from and share in this better world. R.R. Palmer, in his *History of the Modern World,* calls this belief in progress "a kind of nonreligious faith that the conditions of human life" will continually improve as time goes on.

For over a thousand years prior to the seventeenth century, science had progressed little. Inquiry was largely discouraged, and experimentation, almost nonexistent. As a result, science became regressive and discovery was ignored. Benjamin Farrington, a historian of science, characterized it this way: "Science had failed to become a real force in the life of society. Instead there had arisen a conception of science as a cycle of liberal studies for a privileged minority. Science ceased to be a means of transforming the conditions of life." In short, had this intellectual climate continued, humanity's future would have been little more than a clone of its past.

Fortunately, these circumstances were not destined to last. By the seventeenth and eighteenth centuries, Western society was undergoing radical and favorable changes. And the changes that occurred gave rise to the notion that progress was a real force urging civilization forward. Surpluses of consumer goods were replacing substandard living conditions in most of Western Europe. Rigid class systems were giving way to social mobility. In nations like France and the United States, the lofty principles of democracy and popular sovereignty were being painted in broad, gilded strokes over the fading canvasses of monarchy and despotism.

But more significant than these social, economic, and political changes, the new age witnessed a rebirth of science. Centuries of scientific stagnation began crumbling before a spirit of scientific inquiry that spawned undreamed of technological advances. And it was the discoveries and inventions of scores of men and women that fueled these new technologies, dramatically increasing the ability of humankind to control nature—and, many believed, eventually to guide it.

It is a truism of science and technology that the results derived from observation and experimentation are not finalities. They are part of a process. Each discovery is but one piece in a continuum bridging past and present and heralding an extraordinary future. The heroic age of the Scientific Revolution was simply a start. It laid a foundation upon which succeeding generations of imaginative thinkers could build.

It kindled the belief that progress is possible as long as there were gifted men and women who would respond to society's needs. When Antonie van Leeuwenhoek observed *Animalcules* (little animals) through his high-powered microscope in 1683, the discovery did not end there. Others followed who would call these "little animals" bacteria and, in time, recognize their role in the process of health and disease. Robert Koch, a German bacteriologist and winner of the Nobel Prize in Physiology and Medicine, was one of these men. Koch firmly established that bacteria are responsible for causing infectious diseases. He identified, among others, the causative organisms of anthrax and tuberculosis. Alexander Fleming, another Nobel Laureate, progressed still further in the quest to understand and control bacteria. In 1928, Fleming discovered penicillin, the antibiotic wonder drug. Penicillin, and the generations of antibiotics that succeeded it, have done more to prevent premature death than any other discovery in the history of humankind. And as civilization hastens toward the twenty-first century, most agree that the conquest of van Leeuwenhoek's "little animals" will continue.

The Encyclopedia of Discovery and Invention examines those discoveries and inventions that have had a sweeping impact on life and thought in the modern world. Each book explores the ideas that led to the invention or discovery, and, more importantly, how the world changed and continues to change because of it. The series also highlights the people behind the achievements—the unique men and women whose singular genius and rich imagination have altered the lives of everyone. Enhanced by photographs and clearly explained technical drawings, these books are comprehensive examinations of the building blocks of human progress.

RAILROADS

Bridging the Continents

RAILROADS

Introduction

For at least one hundred years, from about 1850 to 1950, the distant wail of a steam locomotive's whistle was one of the world's most romantic sounds. As trains hissed and clicked through countryside and towns, adults stopped working to wave and dream for a moment of riding the rails to some far-off destination. Children ran alongside the tracks, shouting greetings and dreaming of becoming an engineer. Railroads captured everyone's imagination. They symbolized progress and prosperity and provided the first convenient, fast, and safe method of land transportation the world had ever known.

But railroads did more than move people from place to place. Before the railroads were built, news about some-thing as important as the death of a king might take three months to spread across a country as small as England. With a network of railroads established, news traveled to far-flung communities in a matter of days. Before railroads, city dwellers suffered from ill health because they could not get a steady supply of fresh foods from the countryside. The railroads delivered farm-fresh milk and produce to the cities daily. Railroads hauled raw materials to the factories and then delivered the manufactured goods to cities and towns cheaply and regularly. They aided in national defense by providing quick military transport. They united countries by linking isolated areas.

Even more, they helped build nations, as towns, factories, and farms were established along their lines. From the

TIMELINE: RAILROADS

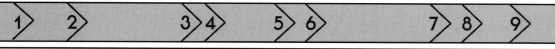

1 ■ 1400s
Mining railways begin in Europe.

2 ■ 1769
World's first steam-driven vehicle is invented in France.

3 ■ 1803
World's first public freight railway begins service in England.

4 ■ 1804
World's first public passenger railway opens in Wales; steam locomotive is invented in England.

5 ■ 1825
World's first railroad begins service in England.

6 ■ 1830
First U.S. railroad opens.

7 ■ 1864
The Pioneer Pullman Car is built.

8 ■ 1869
World's first transcontinental railroad opens in the United States.

9 ■ 1879
Electric locomotive is invented in Germany.

invention of public railroads in 1825 to the end of World War II in 1945, railroads were the king of transportation.

The twentieth century, however, brought new inventions that gave the railroads serious competition. Even before World War II, during the 1920s and 1930s, railroads were threatened by the increasing number of automobiles and trucks that were using an expanding network of paved, public roads. Then, the war ushered in the jet age, and planes quickly became the new king of transportation. In Europe, however, experimentation with new railroad technology continued.

As a result, railroads have thrived in Europe. But in the United States, where distances are long and airfares have traditionally been cheap, most people came to believe that trains are a slow, old-fashioned way to travel. Long-distance passenger trains virtually disappeared after World War II. Many American railroads went bankrupt. Others merged so that they could better compete with trucks for freight traffic. Their success has been limited. In fact, the future of railroads in the United States has been in doubt since the 1950s.

Since the 1980s, however, U.S. railroads are again sparking public interest. In a time of uncertain oil supplies, high gasoline prices, air pollution, and crowded highways, high-speed trains offer an attractive alternative for passenger and freight transport. It is unlikely railroads will ever again be king of transportation, but if given a second chance, they may once again become symbols of progress and prosperity.

10 ■ 1883
Railroad Standard Time goes into effect.

11 ■ 1895
World's first electric railroad begins service in the United States.

12 ■ 1912
Diesel locomotive is invented in Germany.

13 ■ 1934
First streamlined diesel passenger train begins service in the United States.

14 ■ 1964
World's first high-speed railroad opens in Japan.

15 ■ 1970
U.S. Congress creates Amtrak.

16 ■ 1979
World's first *maglev* train is demonstrated in Japan.

17 ■ 1981
France opens the first high-speed *TGV* line.

18 ■ 1990
First *maglev* passenger license given to Las Vegas line.

Gathering the Pieces

Few people in Great Britain realized in 1800 that their small island would soon give birth to the most exciting innovation in land transportation in two thousand years. They would not have believed that people would soon be able to go from London to York in a horseless coach and travel at the unheard-of speed of ten miles an hour. And that would be just the beginning. In a very short time, the new invention would far exceed its creators' dreams and change forever the way people lived and thought.

Early Tracks

The idea of the railroad and the technology that made it possible did not appear suddenly in 1800, of course. They developed slowly over centuries, piece by piece, and involved many people and many changes. The first development

In 1800, few people in Great Britain realized that a new era of transportation was dawning and that the horse and carriage would soon be replaced by the railroad car.

This photograph of Roman ruins in Pompeii, Italy, shows how the Romans built two parallel ruts into their roads to guide the wheels of wagons and chariots.

was railway tracks. The idea of providing a smooth, unobstructed track to guide wheels is very old. The ancient Greeks and Romans built two parallel ruts into some of their roads to guide the wheels of their wagons and chariots. These ruts kept the vehicles from running off the road or bouncing over the rough stone pavement. In most cases, the ruts measured 4 feet, 8.5 inches apart. More than two thousand years later, that same measurement would become the standard gauge, or agreed upon distance between rails, for railroad tracks in most of the developed nations of the world.

After the fall of the Roman empire, the idea of a guided track for wheels seems to have disappeared for centuries. As far as experts know, it did not reappear until sometime in the fifteenth century in the iron mines of western Europe. Tired of trying to push wagons full of heavy metals through the narrow, twisting tunnels and up the mine shaft to the outside, miners built rails out of slender, straight tree trunks. To keep the wagons on the rails, they carved grooves into the middle of the broad, wooden wheels. The first real evidence of this innovation is found in a painting of local industries done in 1513 in the cathedral of Rosnava in Czechoslovakia. By the 1590s, the device had been adopted by miners throughout western Europe.

As soon as railways became common in mines, they began going through a series of changes that would make them more efficient. Some of those changes became an important part of railroad technology. For instance, because the grooved wheels often slipped off the rails, the miners began making flanged wheels. A flange is a rim on the inner edge of the wheel that holds it on the rail and guides it along the track so the vehicle does not have to be steered. The tree-trunk rails, which wore out quickly, were soon replaced by thick, square-cut rails of a hard lumber like oak. But these also deteriorated from constant use. At first, they were repaired by nailing additional planks on top of them. Then, an unknown miner fastened a thin strip of iron, called a plate, on top of the rails at the curves, where the wear was the greatest. This worked so well that soon the entire track was plated. Now, the rails lasted longer, but the iron plates quickly ruined the wooden wheels.

This problem was solved in the 1750s by the introduction of solid iron wheels, which promptly created a new problem. The heavy wheels loosened the nails that held the plates on the rails, causing the plates to tilt or fall off. Finally, in 1789, an Englishman named William Jessop introduced cast-iron rails for use with flanged iron wheels. The need for wood had been eliminated entirely.

Mining Railways

Railways were a great help to miners because they enabled a man or horse to pull 2.5 times more weight than without the rails. But the miners still faced another problem that hindered their work and endangered their lives. The mines, deep in the ground, often became flooded. As it turned out, the solution to this problem also became an impor-

(top) William Jessop introduced cast-iron rails for use with flanged iron wheels in railroad mines.
(bottom) The work of James Watt did much to improve the performance of early steam engines.

tant piece of railroad technology. An English blacksmith named Thomas Newcomen produced a steam engine in 1712 that was used to pump the mines dry. This huge, cumbersome engine was stationary. The energy to make the engine run was produced by using steam from heated water and then using cold water to condense the steam back into a

NEWCOMEN'S STEAM PUMP 1712

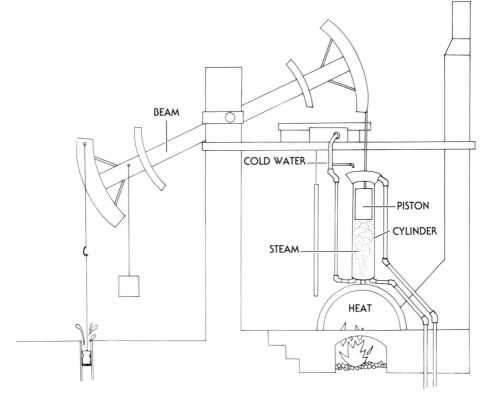

BEAM

COLD WATER

PISTON

CYLINDER

STEAM

HEAT

Thomas Newcomen's steam-engine pump worked on the simple principle that when water is boiled to form steam it expands, and as it cools and condenses into a liquid, it contracts. In Newcomen's steam engine, water inside a sealed cylinder was boiled to form steam. As the steam expanded, it pushed a piston inside the cylinder upward. Then, cold water was sprayed into the cylinder, causing the steam to condense to liquid. This created a vacuum in the cylinder, and sucked the piston back down.

The piston was attached with a rod to one end of a horizontal beam, so it moved up and down with the piston, causing the other end of the beam to move in the opposite direction, like a see-saw. This movement drove the pump, or whatever was attached to the other end of the beam.

liquid. The liquid took up less space than the steam. When the steam condensed in a sealed cylinder, the space left empty became a partial vacuum, which created a sucking action that moved a piston in the cylinder. The piston was attached to one end of a large, horizontal beam that was balanced in the middle like a seesaw. When hot steam was let into the cylinder, it forced the piston up. As the piston rose, so did the end of the beam to which it was attached. At the same time, the other end of the beam sank. That end was also attached to a piston, which operated a pump in the mine. When cold water was sprayed into the cylinder, the steam condensed, and the vacuum sucked the piston down. As that end of the beam was pulled down, the other end was raised, which again moved the piston that operated the pump.

In 1763, when a Scottish engineer named James Watt began to experiment with steam engines, Newcomen's engine was still the best available. But it used a great deal of steam, which meant using a great deal of fuel to heat the water that produced the steam. Also, the alternate heating and cooling of the cylinder wasted a lot of heat. Watt built a more efficient engine by separating the condenser from the cylinder, so that the cylinder would stay hot. This saved three-fourths of the fuel costs. By 1775,

Watt was building more powerful steam engines that not only pumped water out of mines but also drove factory machinery and pumped city water supplies. He continued to build improved engines. But Watt's engines were still large and cumbersome, and had limited power. One reason for this was that Watt always used low-pressure steam, which means he injected only a small amount of steam into the cylinders at one time. The steam pressure in his engines was about fifteen pounds per square inch, which is not much greater than the pressure of the air we breathe. He feared that injecting more steam into the cylinders and creating high pressure would cause an explosion. Because low-pressure engines cannot produce as much power as those operated with high-pressure steam, Watt's engines had limited potential.

The "Trevithick" was constructed by Richard Trevithick in 1802. Trevithick was an enthusiastic builder of steam engines and used higher boiler pressure than had been used in earlier steam engines. Pictured here is one of Trevithick's steam engines.

Putting Steam to Use

Luckily, Watt was not the only person who realized that the steam engine held many possibilities for the future. Watt was a practical man, not a dreamer who was willing to gamble on an invention that seemed farfetched. While he had been improving the steam engine for useful purposes, other men had been working on something that seemed impossible—a road vehicle operated by steam that ran on its own power.

It was a young Frenchman named Nicholas Cugnot who, in 1769, first succeeded in producing such a vehicle. His steam tractor was a heavy, clumsy, three-wheeled vehicle intended to pull field guns for the French army. Actually, it was simply a huge steam engine set on a wooden, wheeled frame. Since the French would not believe the machine could travel by its own power, Cugnot held a public demonstration that year in the streets of Paris. After reaching a speed of nine miles per hour, he was so encouraged by the enthusiasm of the crowd that he began to drive recklessly, despite the fact that he had no brakes. The vehicle turned over and exploded, and the authorities decided Cugnot was a "dangerous lunatic." They put him in prison and impounded his tractor.

In 1784, Englishman William Murdock imitated Cugnot's tricycle design to produce what is called a road locomotive. Murdock was a foreman in James Watt's firm and built his vehicle while staying in Cornwall, in the southwest corner of England, where Watt's steam engines were being installed in tin mines. While he was experimenting with the vehicle one night on a country lane, he lost control of it. As it rolled on down the street without him, it passed by a local priest who was so terrified by the vehicle's steam and smoke that he declared it to be an instrument of the devil. Watt ordered Murdock to stop experimenting. But Murdock's invention did not go unnoticed. A young man named Richard Trevithick recognized Murdock's achievement. Years later, he would succeed where the others had failed.

Steam Vehicles Too Farfetched?

Trevithick was born in Cornwall in 1771. As he grew up, he became fascinated by the steam engines that pumped water out of the mines. By 1800, he had developed a more powerful, high-pressure engine that operated under thirty pounds of pressure and yet was far smaller than Watt's engine. He also invented a more efficient way of moving the pistons. Instead of condensing steam into liquid, Trevithick used only steam to do the job. Because steam expands to take up more space than the liquid that produces it, it builds greater power. He used the power from the expansion of steam to push the pistons and allowed the used steam to escape into the air in puffs. This engine became the model for all later steam engines.

A year after that, Trevithick mounted his engine on a passenger road vehicle. Called *Captain Dick's Puffer,* it was a tricycle with a small front wheel and two large, thin rear wheels. The driver sat just behind the front wheel and steered it with a metal bar. Trevithick first tested it on Christmas Eve in 1801, and it ran well except that the boiler, the container of water that produces the steam, had a tendency to run dry. Three days after firing up the *Puffer*, Trevithick and his friends were still celebrating. Forgetting that the boiler would get thirsty, too, they left the vehicle running outside while they went into an inn for drinks. When they finally rushed out to fill the machine, it was too late. The boiler had run dry, and the vehicle was in flames.

Trevithick was not easily discouraged, so he immediately built a second *Puffer*. In 1803, he took it to London and made a successful run in the city. Unfortunately, neither the roads nor the public was ready for self-powered vehicles. The citizens of London found the idea too farfetched. Trevithick went back to Cornwall and began thinking again. Before long, he came up with the idea of running his steam vehicle on the mining railways, where it could run smoothly and haul the loads of metal more easily than men and horses could. Trevithick's new vehicle was nothing less than a railroad locomotive. A second essential piece of the railroad was now a possibility.

A Timely Idea

Despite the reaction of the general public in London, Trevithick's idea was timely. Other people had also been thinking about the use of the railways. Unlike Trevithick, a mining engineer who planned his invention for the mines, these other people were thinking of money. They saw how the private railways had decreased labor and increased profits for the mines. They thought a public railway might be a profitable new business.

In his 1851 book about the British railways, author John A. Francis described some ideas for creating public railways. In 1800, Francis wrote, a Dr. James Anderson had recommended that a railroad be built for general public use beside the road from London to the resort town of Bath. And, Francis wrote, a Mr. Edgeworth had published a proposal for a public railway in 1802 suggesting that, besides heavy wagons that would go slowly, "stagecoaches might be made to go at six miles an hour, and...gentlemen's travelling carriages at eight—both with one horse."

Although these men and others were thinking of horse-drawn trains, they added a third piece to the blossoming idea of railroads. They wanted railways for the public transport of passengers and freight.

The definition of the term *railroad* reflects all three pieces—the rails, the locomotive, and public availability. A railroad is first and foremost the rolling stock, or a train made up of a mechanically powered locomotive and one or more cars. The train must run on self-guiding rails and be a common carrier, a form of transportation available for a fee to the public for both passage and freight. Additionally, the term *railroad* refers to the company that owns and operates a particular line. In this case, it includes everything from the rolling stock and railways to the employees, buildings, and property.

By the early 1800s, the stage was set for the invention of the railroad. All that remained was to put the various pieces together. This would take time but not the centuries it had taken for the initial ideas and technology to develop. Great Britain was in a hurry.

Putting the Pieces Together

Early nineteenth-century Great Britain was the perfect time and place for the railroad to be born. Seldom before had there been a greater need for improved transportation and communication. For centuries, foot, horseback, and wagons had been the main means of travel. Stagecoaches were introduced in the 1500s for paying passengers, but, in terms of comfort and speed, they were not much better. In summer, passengers almost suffocated from the heat and dust. In winter, they had to endure freezing temperatures. In all seasons, they were constantly jolted and thrown around as the stagecoach slowly lurched along from one stop to another. These hardships often went on for days, because a trip of two hundred miles took about a week.

Roughing It on the Roads

The roads were the primary reason why stagecoach travel was so difficult. When it rained, the horses often sank into the mud up to their bellies. Usually, passengers had to help push the coach out of the mire before they could continue

During the Industrial Revolution, trains were needed to transport manufactured goods from factories such as this one in Germany.

their journey. When the roads dried or froze, the deep holes left by the wheels hardened into a treacherous maze of deep ruts. The resulting jolts threw people out of their seats, broke wheels, and tipped coaches completely over.

Freight transportation had an even harder time on the roads. The heavy wagons, loaded down with coal, tin, or produce from the farms, sank deeper into the mud than the passenger coaches, causing many delays and creating bigger ruts. And in many areas, there were no alternative ways to ship goods. Because of these difficulties, it sometimes cost as much to transport an item by wagon as it did to buy it. In fact, it was cheaper and easier to export goods by ship than to transport them by wagon around the country.

By 1800, the situation had become intolerable. The Industrial Revolution had started in Great Britain around 1760 and ushered in an age of optimism, innovation, and growth that produced many scientific and technological advances. New machines helped people make things much faster than they could by hand. Soon, many items were being manufactured in great quantities in factories located in urban areas.

This created several transportation problems. When people began to move to the cities to work in the factories, for example, it became increasingly difficult to transport enough food from the farms to feed the growing urban population. Another problem was that the factories consumed great quantities of raw materials that had to be brought in from other areas of the country. And then the manufactured goods had to be delivered to the cities, towns, and villages, where people were demanding more of these cheaper items.

The farmers and the factory owners looked around for a solution to their transportation problems, and it was then that they began to take notice of the mining railways. By this time, these private railways had come out of the mines. To get their coal and other minerals to the cities, mine owners had extended their railways to meet canals, and this often involved distances of up to ten miles. These railways, operated with horse-drawn wagons, seemed a perfect answer for hauling many tons of goods and farm produce. The railways, however, were privately owned and therefore not available to anyone else. Then, in about 1800, a group of people in Surrey, a farming district southwest of London, became interested in the proposals being made by Dr. James Anderson and others for public railways. They realized that was the answer.

Railway Horses Pull Their Weight

The Surrey group decided to build a public railway from Wandsworth on the Thames River in London to Croydon, which later became a suburb of London—a distance of about 9.5 miles (15 kilometers). First, however, the promoters had to persuade Parliament to pass an act making the railway legal. That was the only way the group could get permission to buy the land they needed to build the railway. When Parliament did pass the act in 1801, it established the first public railway in history and set a precedent for all public railroads to follow. The first piece of the railroads had been put into place.

The railway, called the Surrey Iron Railway, opened on July 26, 1803, for horse-drawn freight carriers only. Because the owners viewed the railway as a way of boosting their freight delivery profits, passenger travel was never considered. The railway carried Surrey's agricultural produce into London and brought back manure for Surrey's farms. Instead of owning their own rolling stock, the promoters opened the railway, for a toll, to all people who could provide their own horses and wagons. Unfortunately, information on how this first public freight railway fared is not readily available.

Information on the first public passenger railway is even more difficult to find because it was too small to receive much public notice. What is known is that the first public passenger railway, Oystermouth Railway in Wales, was incorporated in 1804, following another act by Parliament. On March 25, 1807, its horse-drawn wagons began carrying paying passengers between Oystermouth and Swansea, a distance of six miles. The railway remained in use, for various purposes, until 1960.

Another reason the Oystermouth Railway may not have received much publicity when it opened is that by then, something much more momentous had happened. The most important piece of the railroads had made its public appearance. In 1804, Richard Trevithick ran the first steam locomotive on rails.

First Steam Locomotive

After Trevithick demonstrated his steam road vehicle in London in 1803, a man named Samuel Homfray, who owned the Penydarren ironworks in South Wales, hired him to build a steam engine for his plant. While Trevithick was there, another ironworks owner named Anthony Hill bet Homfray one thousand pounds that he could not move ten tons of iron on his nine-mile railway from Penydarren to the Glamorganshire Canal without the power of men or horses. This was a considerable sum of money and Homfray urged Trevithick to win the bet for him.

Trevithick was delighted. He loved gambling, and he saw a chance to make his fortune. So he modified the steam engine he had been building and mounted it on wheels. On February 13, 1804, the first steam locomotive began its nine-mile journey down the Penydarren railway, pulling five wagons loaded with a total of ten tons of iron, plus seventy curious passengers who raised the total weight to about fifteen tons. The engine performed well, needing no additional water and traveling at up to five miles per hour. However, the journey took four hours and five minutes because of stops to cut away obstructing trees and remove rocks from the tracks. Homfray won his bet, and Trevithick was triumphant.

Primitive as Trevithick's Penydarren locomotive was, steam locomotives still operate on the same basic principles. The fuel—usually coal but sometimes wood or even oil—is burned in a firebox. The heat from the fire turns the water stored in the adjacent boiler into steam. As the steam accumulates in the boiler, it begins to build up pressure, and the pressure forces the steam up into the steam dome. Not all the steam makes it to the dome. To prevent explosions, the boiler is equipped with a safety valve to let steam off into the air if the pressure becomes too great. And some of the steam, as well as smoke and sparks from the fire, escape into the smoke box and are expelled into the air through the smokestack.

The steam that makes it to the steam dome then travels down through the steam pipe to the cylinders that hold the pistons. The pressure of the steam makes the pistons move back and forth inside the cylinders. It is the sound of the steam pushing the pistons first one way and then another that makes the *choo-choo* sound that steam locomotives are famous for. As the pistons move, the drive rods, connected to the pistons at one end, move back and forth at the same time. The drive rods, in turn, move the connecting rods, which connect the driving wheels. These connecting rods turn the wheels, which keep the locomotive in motion.

By controlling the amount of steam pressure in the cylinders, engineers can control the speed of the locomotive. The more steam pressure there is, the faster the train will go and the more water and fuel the engine will consume. In order to assure a steady supply of fuel and water, a supply car called a tender is attached directly behind the locomotive.

Weight Poses a Problem

The Penydarren locomotive worked so well that it began making regular runs between the ironworks and the canal. But Trevithick's joy did not last long. His locomotive was too heavy for the plated rails. It constantly crushed them, frequently causing the Penydarren to

William Hedley's famous locomotive Puffing Billy *proved that smooth wheels could run on smooth rails.*

derail. Moreover, Homfray's wagon drivers resented the locomotive, fearing it would put them out of work. Afraid of sabotage, Trevithick abandoned his locomotive.

Eventually, Trevithick lost interest in steam locomotion and returned to being a mining engineer. He disappeared from railroad history and never received any financial rewards for his important invention.

After 1810, however, toward the end of the Napoleonic Wars between Great Britain and France, horses to pull wagons and fodder to feed the horses became scarce because they were needed by the army. Steam locomotives again looked attractive, and engineers began a renewed effort to solve the problems Trevithick had faced. Some succeeded in improving the rails, but the heavy locomotives fractured even cast-iron rails. Some tried to make lighter engines, but that created a new problem. A light engine trying to pull a heavy load up a steep grade tended to slide backward down the hill. That made engineers doubt that smooth wheels would work on smooth rails.

Smooth Wheels Run on Smooth Rails

William Hedley, a mining superintendent, solved the problem in 1813 by using gears to apply power from the engine to both the front and back pairs of wheels instead of to just one pair. The result was a famous locomotive called *Puffing Billy* that proved smooth wheels could run on smooth rails. This tiny locomotive, puffing through the countryside and sending

George Stephenson, a brilliant engineer who became known as the "father of English railroads," promoted the use of steam locomotives.

out showers of steam, smoke, and cinders, was a huge success. It was so successful, in fact, that it remained in use for fifty years.

Still, at first, *Puffing Billy* damaged the rails as badly as previous engines had. Within a short time, someone—possibly Timothy Hackworth, foreman of Hedley's blacksmith shop—came up with an answer. He rebuilt the locomotive with four pairs of wheels instead of two, thereby distributing the weight of the engine over eight wheels. With less weight on each wheel, the destruction of the rails ceased. It was not until the invention of much stronger wrought-iron rails in 1830, that the number of wheels could be reduced again to four.

After that success, engineers raced each other to produce better locomotives, and many made improvements that became part of the future technology. But one brilliant man stands out above all the rest. His name was George Stephenson, and he became known as "the father of English railroads." Stephenson was born in 1781, one of six children in a poor family. He never went to school, but because he was determined to become an engineer, he taught himself to read and write and do arithmetic. By the age of seventeen, he had a better mining job than his father. In his twenties, he became obsessed with the potential of steam locomotion, and by 1814, he had persuaded his employer, Lord Ravensworth, to give him financial backing to build a locomotive. Just nine years after building his first locomotive, he had his own steam locomotive factory, called the Stephenson Locomotive Works, in Newcastle-upon-Tyne.

Stephenson's excellent reputation made him a natural choice when a financier named Edward Pease needed an engineer for a new railway project. Pease had been trying since 1810 to persuade Parliament to pass an act allowing the operation of a public freight railway in northern England. The proposal called for wooden rails to convey horse-drawn wagons loaded with "coal, iron, lime, corn and other commodities from the interior of the county of Durham to the town of Darlington and the town and port of Stockton." But when the act was finally passed in 1821, Stephenson was not satisfied with the plans. He persuaded Pease to use iron rails and to work part of the railway with steam locomotives. This required a new act of Parliament. Passed in 1823,

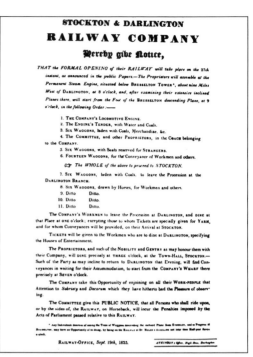

A public notice announces the opening of the Stockton & Darlington Railway, the first public steam-powered railway to carry both freight and passengers.

it authorized both the use of locomotives and passenger service.

The Pieces Come Together

On September 27, 1825, opening day of the Stockton & Darlington Railway (S&D), all the pieces that make up the railroad came together for the first time. The S&D was a public railroad that carried both freight and passengers in a train powered by a steam locomotive that ran on rails. The railroad had been invented.

The opening ceremonies drew curious people from miles around. The bravest walked up close and examined the train with awe. In front, huffing and puffing, was one of Stephenson's newest locomotives, named *Locomotion*. Behind it, stretching far down the track, were thirty-three cars. One car was a private coach for the owners and directors, and the rest consisted of fourteen wagons for workers to stand in, six wagons for passengers to stand in, five wagons to hold coal and passengers, one wagon to hold flour and passengers, and six wagons for just coal. When the time came for the first run, 450 excited passengers squeezed into that limited space.

When *Locomotion* was almost ready to begin huffing its way along the twenty-one-mile (thirty-four-kilometer) run from Shilton to Stockton, a horse rider dressed in the formal white pants, red jacket, and black hat of a coachman and carrying a red flag pranced out onto the track in front of the engine. It was his job to lead the locomotive down the track as a precaution against any mishaps. With apprehension, the spectators watched as Stephenson built up steam in the engine. Suddenly, the safe-ty valve lifted, letting out a surge of steam with a fearsome hiss. Men, women, and children ran for their lives, convinced there was going to be an explosion. But their fear was soon forgotten when the train began moving.

As the train glided slowly down the tracks behind the horse, people running alongside jumped up to hitch a ride on this marvelous new invention. By the end of the run, the train was carrying six hundred passengers and weighed a total of ninety tons. Despite the added weight, *Locomotion* performed perfectly. In fact, Stephenson got impatient with the slow speed of the horse and finally motioned for the rider to get out of the way. At points during the rest of the run, he reached a speed of somewhere between fifteen and twenty miles per hour.

Although the S&D was never an important railroad, it proved to the world that the new invention had valuable potential. Suddenly, every industrialist wanted to build a railroad.

The Railroad Arrives: Railroad Mania

By the time the railroad was invented in 1825, the Industrial Revolution was reaching its peak in Great Britain. The new industrialists owned factories and they had developed into a wealthy, powerful class of society along with many merchants and other people in commerce. Their goal was to become even more wealthy and powerful. With this in mind, they began to keep a close eye on the S&D and other railroads that followed. Very soon, the railroads looked like the perfect new machine to aid in their money-making schemes. They could see that railroads moved goods and raw materials more cheaply, quickly, and reliably than wagons or canals.

The railroads would allow the industrialists to increase profits by producing and selling more. Before the S&D, for example, Stockton had exported 1,224 tons of coal. In 1828, only three years after the railroad opened, Stockton exported 66,051 tons. They could also see that building and operating a railroad was a good way to make money.

Within a year after the S&D opened, the people who had backed it financially were making a 5 percent profit on their money. Within just a few more years, they were making 13 percent. The railroad was definitely the road to riches. But, in the beginning, it would not be a smooth one. As it turned out, the industrialists were the only people who wanted the railroads.

Fear Fights the Railroad

The troubles had begun before the S&D opened, when only a few insightful industrialists were pioneering the building of railroads. The efforts to build a line from the city of Manchester to the port in the city of Liverpool, a distance of thirty-one miles, reveal the difficulties they had to overcome. Immediately after the Liverpool-Manchester Railroad (L&M) was proposed, the landowners, farmers, and canal and stagecoach companies in the area began a fierce fight against it. Knowing that the railroads would eventually drive them out of business, the canal and stagecoach companies began to spread stories that exaggerated the fears of the general public about railroads. The public, knowing only that a locomotive was a frightening, noisy thing that went faster than anything ever seen before, tended to believe those stories.

The landowners believed that their land would be ruined and that the air would become so polluted with smoke that all living things would die. Farmers believed that sparks from the smokestack would burn their barns, haystacks, and cottages, and that their cows would stop giving milk. Other citizens believed that the speed of the train would cause people to explode or go mad or, at the very least, go blind and deaf. They talked about how horses would become extinct, and of how passengers would suffocate

EARLY STEAM LOCOMOTIVES

Englishman George Stephenson's *Rocket*, built in 1829, featured all of the basic parts of the steam locomotive. The *Rocket* proved that locomotives were fast, reliable, and relatively inexpensive. It used a double-action steam engine, like the one invented by James Watt. Small boiler tubes that ran through the boiler produced steam quickly. The hottest and driest steam rose to the steam dome, and from there it was carried through steampipes to the two diagonal cylinders. Each cylinder contained a piston that was attached directly by a drive rod and connecting rod to one of the two drive wheels.

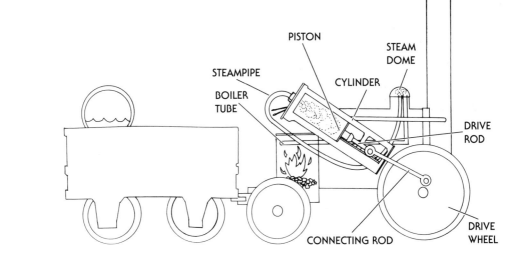

in tunnels. Even the Duke of Wellington, who beat Napoleon at the Battle of Waterloo and became the prime minister of Great Britain, felt that the railroads were dangerous. But his reason was somewhat different. He felt they would allow the lower classes, whom he considered radicals and troublemakers, to travel freely about the country, stirring up rebellion against the ruling class.

The uproar caused by these fears worked. Parliament refused to approve the first L&M proposal in 1824. When Parliament finally did approve a second proposal in 1826, it was rumored that the reason was a very large bribe. But the troubles were not over. Landowners and canal and stagecoach companies hired lawyers to fight the railroad legally and gangs of roughnecks to fight its surveyors illegally. Bridges over canals were torn down in the night. Building the L&M was a nightmare for George Stephenson, who had been hired as the engineer. And even when the railway was near completion, the promoters still had not decided it was wise to use steam locomotives instead of horses. Public opinion was against it, and most people did not think steam power was reliable.

Stephenson's Rocket *locomotive proved the potential of steam-powered trains.*

Testing Their Mettle

Stephenson argued so persuasively for the use of locomotives that the promoters agreed to hold a public contest with a prize of money to the winner. If any locomotive could prove its value in speed, reliability, and cost, they would use locomotives on the railroad. As a result, a famous event in railroad history called the Rainhill Trials began on October 6, 1829, before about ten thousand spectators. The guidelines for the locomotives entered were very strict. Among other conditions, they could not weigh more than six tons or cost over a certain amount. And the locomotives had to be able to pull twenty tons at a steady ten miles per hour for the equivalent of thirty miles.

Five locomotives entered the contest. One was disqualified because a horse was found inside it. Two of the others broke down, and the fourth could not get up to speed. Only one locomotive, the *Rocket,* built by Stephenson and his son Robert, fulfilled all the requirements. In fact, it exceeded them by traveling with a lightened load at the unheard-of speed of twenty-nine miles per hour. The *Rocket* proved once and for all the value of steam locomotives. From that point on, they would be unstoppable.

On opening day of the L&M, September 15, 1830, fifty thousand spectators came to see the ceremonies, despite the gray skies and periodic downpours. The Rainhill Trials had received a lot of publicity, and even people who were scared of the locomotives wanted to see this marvel for themselves. While soldiers and railroad police held back the crowds, eight trains made the thirty-one mile trip. Each carried one hundred elegantly dressed passengers, including politicians who had fought against the L&M. The Duke of Wellington officiated. His train was decorated with silk flags and powered by a new locomotive called *Northumbrian,* and it pulled out of the station to the tune of "See the Conquering Hero Comes" played by three bands.

Halfway down the track, the *Northumbrian* stopped at Parkside to take on water. The passengers, although warned not to disembark, got off to see the locomotive. Suddenly, the *Rocket,* pulling another train, appeared on the second of the two parallel tracks. Everyone scrambled to get out of the way, but William Huskisson, a member of Parliament, did not make it. The *Rocket* hit him, and he died that night. Despite this death, and the fact that someone tried unsuccessfully to derail another train named *Comet* by putting a wheelbarrow on the track, the

L&M was a total success. The railroad had arrived. The L&M was the first all-steam common carrier in the world. It had specialized passenger and freight stations and operated on a timetable. Within fourteen days, the L&M was carrying eight hundred passengers a day; within a few years, it was twelve hundred a day. And the promoters had doubled the money they had invested.

Building Frenzy

By this time, industrialists were rushing to form railroad companies and finance them by selling stock to investors. The stock was simply a certificate that entitled the buyer to a share in later profits in return for investing money to get the company started. Parliament was besieged with proposals for acts to build railroads, and tracks began appearing all over the country. By 1836, proposals had been made for almost every possible practical line: 450 had been completed, and 350 more were in progress.

Gradually, the proposals became more and more absurd. As the large number of companies fought each other for profits, as many as four competing lines were built between two cities. In one small district, sixteen lines were proposed that would have required the destruction of twelve hundred houses. Another line proposed destroying the London docks. Parliament had the good sense to stop some of the more ridiculous proposals, but the rush for profits continued.

This building frenzy made stock in new railroads very popular. By the 1840s, the public's desire to purchase stock in the hope of making a fortune

The Rocket *won the historic Rainhill Trials of 1829.*

Poor passengers rode in open wagons that ran on rails. An early rail car, shown on the right, was propelled by the wind.

was so great that the craze has been labeled railroad mania. Factory workers, farm wives, shop girls, carriage drivers, members of Parliament, and lords and dukes fought each other for the op-

Coaches mounted on rails were the first "passenger trains."

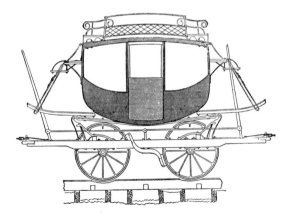

portunity to buy stock. Many did make a fortune, but just as many others went bankrupt. Too many competing lines meant that some companies failed. And toward the end of the 1840s, when the mania was at its height, many unscrupulous people saw a way to make their fortune at the expense of the public by selling stock for nonexistent railroads. Eventually, the absurdity and dishonesty put an end to the mania, and by 1850, reason had returned. Many of the competing companies merged, and a useful network of railroad lines was formed.

While railroad mania was overtaking the country, the railroad industrialists had only two things in mind: profits and freight. Carrying passengers was not their primary concern but was simply a burden they had to bear. Consequently, traveling by train was burdensome. Even the first-class passengers did not have a comfortable ride. The early first-class carriages or coaches were basically horse coaches mounted on flanged wheels. (Passenger cars are still called coaches or carriages.) The seats were uncomfortable, and there was no lighting, heating, or toilet facilities. Luggage was stowed on top of the coach, where it was in danger of catching on fire from sparks. For the very wealthy and the aristocrats, there was an alternative. They could travel in style in their own carriages, complete with footman on top, by paying to have them loaded on flatcars with blocks of wood securing the wheels.

The second- and third-class passengers had no alternatives. Second-class passengers rode in wagons that had roofs but sometimes no sides. When the wagons did have sides, often there were no windows. Some seats were provided, but when the train was crowded, many passengers had to stand, and there was no place for the luggage. But compared to the third-class cars, that was luxurious. Third-class passengers stood in open boxes, sixty to a box, with nothing but their umbrellas to protect them from the elements. Since many journeys took hours, they must have suffered incredible hardships.

In 1844, Parliament took pity on passengers, particularly those in third class, and passed an act requiring, among other things, roofs and sides on all wagons. Gradually, as passengers began to bring in more and more profits, the railroads introduced some improvements on their own. In 1838, the London and Birmingham Railroad introduced the "bed carriage," the forerunner of the sleeping car. By means of hinged seat backs and cushions propped on poles, the seats of an

Third-class railway carriages were very crowded, each holding as many as sixty passengers.

Sleeping cars, or "bed carriages," were introduced in 1838.

ordinary first-class coach compartment converted into two beds. By 1839, first-class coaches were lighted And after a murder in one of the coaches, communication cords were installed so passengers could signal the engineer. But most improvements were not made until 1846. One for which the passengers were particularly grateful was the introduction of food service at the stations.

Excitement Builds and Spreads

Regardless of the hardships, more and more passengers of all classes rode the trains. Railroads gave people a mobility unknown before. The unemployed could travel farther from home to seek jobs. Even the marriage market broadened when people had access to cheap transportation away from their farms and villages. And for the first time, almost everyone could afford to take vacations. Cheap day excursions were

available even to the poor. Thomas Cook, a former gardener's helper, began the world's first travel agency by arranging day excursions on the railroad in 1841.

Increased mobility was only one of the consequences railroads brought to British society. Not all the effects were positive. Railroads hastened the growth of cities by making it easy for people to move to them. A whole new class of urban poor, who lived in filth and squalor, developed in the industrial areas. But the positive effects seemed to outweigh the disadvantages.

Because more and more people were taking vacations, seaside resorts like Brighton on England's southern coast sprang up almost overnight. Other new towns grew up along the lines to provide services to the railroad and passengers. Farmers found broader markets and had ready access to new technology to increase their output, which, in turn, provided more fresh food to the cities. In fact, everyone had easier access to all kinds of information, as the railroads hastened the delivery of mail, newspapers, and gossip. The railroads put a heavy demand on the coal and metal industries, and in response, the technology in those fields developed quickly to keep pace. These advances, combined with the speed and efficiency the railroads provided, helped push the Industrial Revolution to its fullest potential. By 1850, Great Britain had become the "workshop of the world." One of its most valuable exports, the railroad, was spreading around the globe at the rate of one hundred miles a day.

Many countries embraced the railroad as the answer to their transportation problems, but none more enthusiastically than the budding new United States. There was some opposition, particularly from stagecoach and canal companies whose business was threatened by railroads. On the whole, though, railroads seemed the perfect answer to some of the young nation's most pressing problems.

One of the main concerns of the government was how to build and maintain national unity in a huge country with a widely scattered population. The railroad would provide the necessary communication links. National defense was another problem. Americans had recently won their independence and wanted to protect it. The railroad would permit quick movement of troops and supplies to a threatened area. And, perhaps most important, Americans wanted to develop their nation, to move their society westward and bring the rest of the vast land under their control. The railroad would be able to lead the way, for once a line was built into the wilderness, the people would follow.

Passenger Trains Come to the United States

The development of railroads in the United States was quicker than in Great Britain because of technology borrowed from the British. The first wooden rails did not appear until 1795, but the first true railroad with regularly scheduled

Trains improved the speed and efficiency of mail delivery.

passenger service opened on Christmas Day in 1830. On that day, the South Carolina Canal and Railroad Company (SCC&R) ran its locomotive, *Best Friend of Charleston,* on the six miles of track that had been completed. Behind the engine ran a flag-draped flatcar carrying a cannon and three men who fired it continually. Behind that came two wagons carrying more than 140 Charleston socialites.

Best Friend continued to provide regular passenger service for six months, reaching speeds of twenty-five miles per hour. But it met an untimely end on June 7, 1831, when the worker responsible for feeding fuel and water to the engine got tired of listening to the loud hissing of the safety valve and either tied it down or sat on it. Predictably, the boiler blew up, destroying the locomotive and breaking the man's hip.

For some time after that, the SCC&R, obviously expecting more explosions, ran a car loaded with bales of cotton between the tender and the passenger cars. Despite this, the railroad was successful, and when all 136 miles between Charleston and Hamburg,

South Carolina, were finally completed in October 1833, it was the longest continuous length of railway in the world.

The success of the SCC&R and other early railroads, plus the news of the railroad's success in Great Britain, brought railroad mania to the United States. When President Andrew Jackson made the first presidential train trip in 1833, the last of the opposition faded. The railroads spread so fast that by 1835, half of the world's railroads were in the United States. In 1830, there were only twenty-three miles of rails. By 1840, there were twenty-eight hundred miles belonging to 409 railroad companies. By 1850, there were almost nine thousand miles.

Adapting to Different Needs

The U.S. railways were not as well built as those in Great Britain. For one thing, money for investment was limited. Also, the railways had to cover immense distances, often through the wilderness. As a result, American railroads differed

The Best Friend of Charleston *was the first American passenger locomotive to provide regularly scheduled service.*

The "Best Friend," the First Locomotive built in the United States for actual service on a Railroad.

The "BEST FRIEND" was built at the West Point Foundery Shops, in New York City, for the South Carolina Railroad, arrived in Charleston by ship Niagara October 23d, and after several experimental trials, in November and December, 1830, made the first excursion trip, as above, on Saturday, 15th January, 1831, being the anniversary of the commencement of the road. (See extract from *Charleston Courier,* page 252.)

from those in the rest of the world almost from the start. The engineers did not want to take the time to make tunnels and embankments that would help them avoid steep hills and sharp curves. They did not want to bother fastening rails solidly into the ground to keep them level and even. They just wanted to build as quickly and cheaply as possible, which created problems. The biggest one was that unless they went very slowly, locomotives derailed frequently. This led to the development of a new kind of rolling stock.

In 1832, John Jervis, then chief engineer of the Mohawk & Hudson Railroad, modified a British locomotive into what became known as the American type. Instead of four wheels, the American locomotive had eight wheels, four of which were attached to something called a leading truck. This was a separate undercarriage attached to the front end of the locomotive by a swivel. The truck turned independently, leading the locomotive around the curves, and was flexible enough to maintain stability on uneven tracks. American locomotives were also bigger than their British counterparts because their size was not restricted by the size of established tunnels.

The rest of the rolling stock, the freight and passenger cars, also grew bigger because the leading trucks provided stability and a smooth ride to large cars. Larger cars were needed because passenger and freight traffic increased rapidly. By 1832, train travel was so popular that the railroads wanted to run trains at night. The difficulty was that locomotives did not have headlights. The first attempt to solve this problem was made by Horatio Allen, then chief engineer for the SCC&R. He

President Andrew Jackson made the first presidential train trip in 1833.

placed two flatcars in front of a locomotive and built a bonfire of pine knots on a bed of sand on the first one. On the second, he put a piece of polished sheet iron to act as a reflector. It did not work very well, but it was a start. The first headlight that really worked was a whale-oil lamp installed in a locomotive in 1840. It was encased in a metal box that was backed by a tin reflector.

A Place in the Heart

Americans loved their trains and were proud of them. Unlike the British, who built their stations on the outskirts of the cities, away from the homes of the rich, the Americans built their tracks as a main street and put their stations right in the center of town. Since the tracks were never fenced in, they were a source of some danger to the residents. In response, steam whistles were added to locomotives as a warning device. The

(top) Railroad stations, such as this one in Pennsylvania, became centers of activity in the 1800s.
(bottom) Settlers near the Humboldt River eagerly await the arrival of the train.

arrival of a train was a big event, especially in small towns, and people came running when they heard an approaching whistle. In time, each engineer developed a unique personal whistle signal so people could tell which train was coming.

The unfenced track led to problems in the countryside, too. Animals wandered onto the tracks and were killed by the locomotives. Often, locomotives were derailed by cows and even large pigs. In 1833, New Jersey railroad mechanic Isaac Dripps put two pointed iron rods on the front of a locomotive called *John Bull*. He hoped the rods would push the animals off the tracks, but instead the rods speared them.

THE STEAM LOCOMOTIVE IN 1845

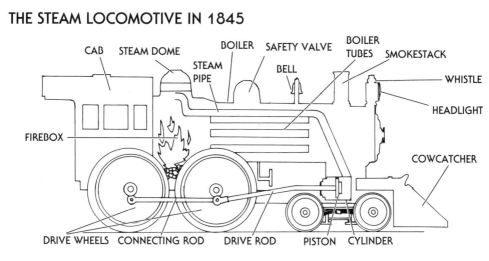

By 1845, the steam locomotive had come a long way. Later locomotives would be bigger, faster, and more powerful, but they had the same essential features: The cylinders and pistons were positioned horizontally in front of the drive wheels, of which there were usually four—two on each side. The engineer and the fireman, who stoked the firebox with coal, stood inside a cab. By 1845, the locomotive also had several new safety features, including a bell, a steam whistle, a headlight, and a cowcatcher, which pushed cattle and other animals clear of the track if they were struck by the locomotive.

After several other attempts to solve the problem, he put a large, wedge-shaped piece of metal on the front of the leading truck. This cowcatcher worked so well, it became standard equipment on American locomotives. The *John Bull* is the oldest existing locomotive in the United States and is on permanent display in the Smithsonian Institution in Washington, D.C.

The railroad owners made a point of saying their trains were built for the public good, and as a result, passengers were treated better than British passengers from the beginning. That does not mean the passengers had no discomforts. The coaches were enclosed, and the only ventilation was through open windows, which allowed soot, smoke, and dust to blow in. Travelers still sat on hard, wooden benches, but they were provided with coal- or wood-burning stoves during the winter. Even sleeper cars appeared in the early 1830s. These had three shelves running the length of the car on both sides. The shelves had partitions every five to six feet that divided them into bunks. Since there were no curtains, passengers slept in their clothes.

The most impressive early development, however, was the rapid expansion of railroad lines through the wilderness. In the 1840s, five railroads met the challenge of crossing the Appalachian Mountains, thereby linking the East Coast to the Midwest. By the 1850s, railroads had reached Chicago and the Mississippi River. These lines carried pioneers and immigrants

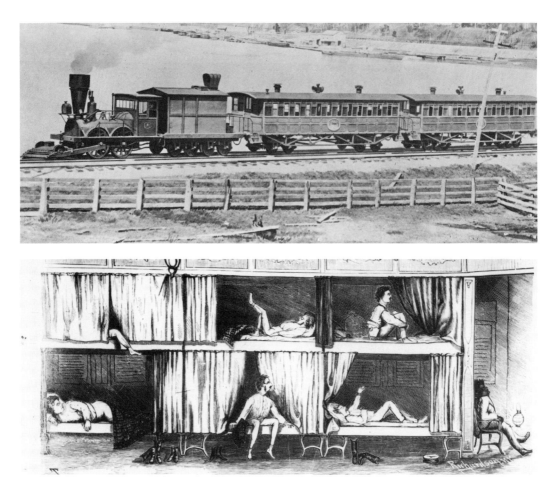

(top) The locomotive John Bull *was the first to employ a cowcatcher on the front car.*
(bottom) Sleeping cars became popular as trains traveled greater distances.

who settled down to farm the new land, and the Midwest began to shimmer with the golden wheat that would later earn it the title of "the nation's breadbasket."

A network of railroads now criss-crossed almost the entire nation east of the Mississippi River, but the biggest challenge lay ahead. Americans were starting to dream of something that seemed impossible: a transcontinental railroad that reached all the way from the Atlantic Ocean to the Pacific Ocean.

Opening the West

A few farsighted Americans were proposing a transcontinental railroad as early as 1832. But building a line through such isolated, rugged terrain was impossible for many years. Then, three things happened that made the difficulties less important. In 1846, the United States took California away from Mexico. Three years later, news of the California gold rush reached the East. Just one year after that, in 1850, California was granted statehood. Suddenly, the population on the Pacific coast be-

Secretary of War Jefferson Davis proposed a southern route for the transcontinental railroad.

gan to grow, and the government again became concerned about national unity and defense. The new state was completely isolated from the East.

Searching for Transcontinental Routes

In 1853, the federal government decided to act. It ordered Secretary of War Jefferson Davis to survey five transcontinental routes—one northern, two central, and two southern. Davis, a rich Southerner, set out to prove that the southernmost route was the best. Despite the fact that the route dipped below the Mexican border, that is the route his final reports recommended.

The young army engineers assigned to survey the land fought blizzards, scorching desert sun, and Native American Indians angered by the taking of their land. But these engineers were not the only ones struggling to complete such a task in the 1850s. Two remarkable young men had each determined to find a route that would make the railroad possible. In California, Theodore Judah was convinced he could find a route over the Sierra Nevada mountains. He persuaded seven men to invest thirty-five thousand dollars to pay for part of his survey. Among those men were two partners in a hardware store named Collis Huntington and Mark Hopkins, a wholesale grocer named Leland Stanford, and a dry goods dealer named

Hardware store owner Mark Hopkins was one of four investors in the western survey for the transcontinental railroad.

Charles Crocker. Judah's survey was successful, and those four men would soon own the rights to his route and would become known as the Big Four.

Meanwhile, in the Midwest, the second young man, Grenville Dodge, spent five years privately surveying a route from Omaha, Nebraska, toward Utah. Soon afterward, while in Council Bluffs, Iowa, he was introduced to a lawyer named Abraham Lincoln, who was himself a railroad enthusiast. Lincoln was curious about the survey, so Dodge told him about his route.

The years slipped by while the government did nothing about the transcontinental railroad. Then, in 1861, the Civil War erupted. Jefferson Davis became president of the Confederate States of America, and his southern route was abandoned. Dodge joined the

Union army and was made a general within two years, and Judah continued to campaign for the railroad. The time was right. The Civil War made national unity an immediate concern.

On July 1, 1862, President Lincoln signed the Pacific Railroad Act. It said that two railroads would be built, one eastward from Sacramento, California, using Judah's route, and the other westward from Omaha, Nebraska, using Dodge's route. The meeting place was not specified.

To help finance the railroads, the government agreed to give the builders ten miles of land along the route for each mile of track laid. Those blocks of land were to alternate with equal blocks of land that would stay under government ownership. The railroads were also

Wholesale grocer Leland Stanford owned part of the rights to the western route of the transcontinental railroad.

granted government loans of between sixteen thousand and forty-eight thousand dollars per mile, depending on the terrain. The Big Four named the railroad starting in Sacramento the Central Pacific (CP). The one out of Omaha was named the Union Pacific (UP).

Pushing the Railroads Through

The Big Four were extraordinary men, and before their railroad was finished, all of them would be extraordinarily wealthy. They were among the most daring businessmen in U.S. history. Although they were perhaps greedy and unscrupulous, the transcontinental railroad would not have been built without them.

By January 8, 1863, ground-breaking day for the Central Pacific, Leland Stanford was governor of California. A heavy, hearty man, Stanford dressed impressively and spoke haltingly, with serious pauses between his words. This made him seem wise and sincere. As president of the CP, he contributed political and administrative skills. Collis Huntington, the vice-president, was a severe, determined workaholic. He spent most of his time in the East, drumming up money to keep the CP going. The treasurer, Mark Hopkins, was a frail, soft-spoken man with two interests: his vegetarian diet and driving a hard bargain. He saw to it that the money Huntington received was well spent. The fourth man, Charles Crocker, did not seem compatible with his partners. Tactless, loud, and profane, Crocker weighed 265 pounds and loved to drink and boast. As construction chief of the CP, his courage and boundless energy

(top) Grenville M. Dodge surveyed a train route from Omaha to Utah.
(bottom) As a young lawyer, Abraham Lincoln showed enthusiasm for Dodge's proposal.

the East around Cape Horn, at the tip of South America. The trip took up to six months. This made it very difficult to keep enough equipment on hand, especially since tools did not last long when used against the hard granite of the Sierra Nevadas. The CP had gone only thirty-four miles out of Sacramento before it reached the granite foothills. The workers would have to blast and dig their way through the high, rugged mountain range by hand.

Hiring Help

At first, the workers themselves were the biggest problem. There simply were not enough of them. Nobody wanted to tackle the hard, dangerous work of building a railroad when they could make more money as a storekeeper or by mining for gold or silver. Mostly because of the labor shortage, it took until March 1865 to extend the railroad fifty-six miles, and the hardest work lay ahead. Crocker was getting desperate.

would get the railroad built, even under the most difficult circumstances.

The problems Crocker faced were horrendous. All the rails, rolling stock, and hardware had to be shipped from

Charles Crocker (above) had the difficult job of managing the construction of the western half of the transcontinental railroad. Labor crews (right) lay tracks for the transcontinental railroad. One crew completed more than ten miles of track in one day.

More than six thousand Chinese laborers helped lay the track from California to Utah.

Then he had an idea. His Chinese servant, Ah Ling, had been loyal, capable, and hard working for years, and California was full of Chinese people who had come to the United States because of the gold strikes. He hired a crew of fifty Chinese immigrants, and they performed so well that more were hired. By the beginning of 1866, six thousand Chinese workers were toiling on the line.

Even with the help of the Chinese laborers, the work in the treacherous mountains was slow. By November 23, 1866, the CP had gone only ninety-two miles, whereas the Union Pacific, advancing from the east across the flat prairie, had progressed 293 miles. Delighted, the UP issued a statement boasting it would reach the California-Nevada border before the CP did. Crocker was furious. That winter, he decided, he would not stop work as he had done the previous winters. Unfortunately for Crocker and his laborers,

the winter of 1866 and 1867 was dreadful. The people who lived through it talked about it for years. There were forty-four blizzards, one of which lasted for thirteen days. Supplies could not get through, so the work crews often had to live on starvation rations. Frequent avalanches buried unrecorded numbers of workers. Snowdrifts reached sixty feet, and living quarters were buried, but the workers scurried to and from work in tunnels dug under the snow.

All through this, the work never stopped, night or day, even though the crews were now at the highest, most exposed point of their job. They were digging the Summit Tunnel, the last, longest, and highest of six tunnels needed to reach the summit of the Sierra Nevadas. At the same time, crews were working on the nine tunnels that would take the railroad down the steep eastern slope of the mountains onto the Nevada desert. Work inside the tunnel, which proceeded from both ends at the same

The railroads had difficulty finding enough laborers for the demanding task of laying tracks.

time, was extremely difficult, because drilling a hole in the hard granite for the blasting powder was slow, tedious work. It was so tedious, in fact, that it took twenty-four hours to blast away eight inches of rock. By August 1867, however, the two crews had met in the middle of Summit Tunnel, and by November, its rails had been laid. The worst was over. From now on, the work would be a lot easier.

Hard Work Progresses

The Union Pacific got off to an even slower start. Although the ground breaking took place in December 1863, the first rail was not laid until July 10, 1865. General Dodge was to become the construction chief, but in 1865, he was still in the army, fighting Indians on the plains. Dodge finally retired

from the army in 1866 and joined the railroad. In the meantime, his foreman, Gen. Jack Casement, handled the construction. General Casement was only five feet, four inches tall, and even with a full beard, he looked like a twelve-year-old. But he was an excellent leader who inspired loyalty in his workers, even though he drilled them like military troops.

Lack of workers was a problem for the UP also. Most men were fighting in the Civil War. By the end of 1865, only forty miles of track had been laid. But when the war ended, the veterans started drifting west, looking for work. Most of the laborers who ended up on the UP were Irish immigrants, but there were also other immigrants, freed slaves, and even Indian women. General Casement drilled them to work as a team, and from 6:30 A.M. to sundown, except for lunch hour, there was a scene of continuous, coordinated motion.

Far ahead of the track crew, perhaps as much as three hundred miles, the surveyors were finalizing the route. Behind them followed the grading crews, who used horses, mules, dump carts, and scrapers to level out hills and hollows. They formed the flat, narrow, earth-and-gravel roadbed for the track. Then came the bridge crews, erecting wooden bridges over rivers and gullies. They were followed by the tie men, who laid the wooden crossties on the roadbed. The ties were sent by wagon from forests near the Rocky Mountains, where other gangs of workers were busy cutting down trees to make them. The track crew came last, usually about twenty miles behind the rest, and worked under the always watchful eye of General Casement.

First thing in the morning, horse-drawn rail carts were positioned next to a pile containing all the supplies needed by the track crew that day. Six workers quickly loaded each cart with sixteen rails, plus the proper number of

The Sioux and Cheyenne Indians fought to prevent the railroad from crossing their lands.

spikes, bolts, and rail couplings. Then the horses pulled the carts at a run to the very end of the rail laid the previous day. Immediately, the rails were unloaded two at a time with five-man teams handling each rail. The cart was tipped over off the track so the next cart could

Railroad labor crews frequently battled with Indians.

In the meantime, each five-man team rushed to hold its rail in position over the crossties, until the rail boss gave the order to lower it. The minute the rails were down, workers with gauges spaced them exactly 4 feet, 8.5 inches apart. When the gaugers shouted, "Ready," the spike men hammered in the spikes that attached the rails to the crossties. This work was so well coordinated that with ten spikes to the rail and three blows to each spike, two rail lengths were laid each minute.

Obstacles Threaten Success

Aside from furious winter and summer storms in the prairies, there were two main obstacles to maintaining this pace of work. The first was the Indians who lived along the route. Some Indian tribes accepted the railroad, but the

deliver its load, and when the track was free, the cart was replaced on the track and rushed back for another load.

Scout and Indian fighter William F. Cody (above), also known as Buffalo Bill, supplied the railroad crews with buffalo meat. The temporary towns (right) that popped up across the prairie offered gambling and entertainment to the laborers. These wild, mobile towns became known as "hells on wheels."

Sioux and the Cheyenne had fifteen thousand braves who were ready to die to keep it off their land. At first, the Indians tried to discourage the crews by stealing supplies and stampeding the horses and mules. But that soon escalated to attacks on the work crews and the locomotives. General Casement drilled his workers until they could defend themselves like an army with the rifles kept ready in the work train, but many railroad workers and Indians died in the coming battles.

The Indians were up against a power they did not understand, and they did not know how to fight it. One war party of fifty braves attempted to capture a moving locomotive. The braves split up into twenty-five teams of two, and each pair, with one man on either side of the track, strung a lariat between their horses so it stretched across the track. When the locomotive hit those rawhide lariats at twenty-five

miles per hour, the braves nearest the rails and their horses were thrown into the wheels and dismembered.

General Dodge, by this time, was storming up and down the line, leaving no doubt as to who was in charge. He used his influence to get more and more military troops sent to protect his railroad. By 1868, there were five thousand soldiers patrolling the miles between the surveyors and the rail crews. Badly outnumbered and outgunned, the Indians could do nothing to stop the railroad from moving ahead.

The second obstacle to fast construction was one shared with the Central Pacific. Supplies had to come from the East, up the Missouri River by boat, and across the plains by wagon. The route was slow and uncertain, and this was a particular problem when food for the workers was delayed. The answer to the food shortage came in the form of a tall, handsome scout and

Union Pacific vice president Thomas Durant joined Leland Stanford in commemorating the completion of the railroad.

Indian fighter named William F. Cody. In 1867 and 1868, he contracted with the railroad to provide buffalo meat for five hundred dollars a month. Cody brought them ten to twelve buffalo per day for eighteen months.

As the work progressed, it seemed that every sixty miles or so along the roadbed, a temporary town would appear. The ratty tents and buildings contained people who wanted to take the workers' pay, including gamblers, saloon keepers, con men, and prostitutes. Every night, the noise of music, joking, dancing, swearing, and shooting filled the town. Almost every morning, there would be a burial of someone killed in the drunken spree. In one of these towns, thirty-eight people were killed in three months; in another, twenty-eight were killed in one month. When the railroad construction moved past the town, the people would pack up their tents, dismantle their buildings, and move another sixty miles or so up the roadbed. Because of this, these towns were called "hells on wheels."

Nearing Completion

By 1868, the CP was proceeding rapidly across the Nevada desert, but the UP still had to face its biggest challenge, the Rocky Mountains and the Wasatch Mountains in Utah. Although the CP had been forced to build fifteen tunnels in the Sierra Nevada, the UP had to build only four. It was obvious that the transcontinental railroad would indeed be completed, and, more than ever, the two railroads competed to see which could lay the most track.

The competition was not simply a matter of pride. The government land grants and loans given for every mile of track laid made it a matter of economics. In fact, a great deal of money was at stake. By the beginning of 1869, both railroads were racing toward each other in Utah. It was obvious neither had any intention of stopping. Actually, they did not know where they were supposed to stop. The government had never designated a meeting place. Finally, the two railroads met in the desert. And they kept on going. The two parallel lines swept past each other, so close that the blasting was a danger to the other line's crews.

Both railroads continued to build, side by side, for more than two hundred miles, until the secretary of the interior, Orville Browning, decided to stop it. He appointed a commission of engineers to go to Utah and decide where the meeting place should be. On April 10, 1869, Congress announced that the two railroads would meet at Promontory Point on the northern shore of Great Salt Lake in Utah. Now that there was no more money to be gained, the race stopped. The UP had laid 1,085 miles of track; the CP had laid 690. The total cost of the transcontinental railroad would be $165 million, of which the U.S. government would contribute $65 million.

On April 28, the tracks were so close to meeting that May 8 was set as the official meeting date. A big ceremony was planned, and important railroad officials would attend. The highlight of the ceremony would come when Leland Stanford, president of the CP, and Dr. Thomas Durant, vice-president of the UP, used a silver-headed hammer to drive in the last spike, which was made of solid gold.

This was the biggest news story since the end of the Civil War. Newspaper reporters and two photographers would be present. Telegraph wires were to be fastened to both the gold spike and the silver hammer, so the news of completion of the first transcontinental railroad would be sent electrically throughout the country. In Washington, D.C., the signal would drop a ball placed on the dome of the Capitol. In San Francisco, it would ring the tower bell in City Hall. In New York, the choir of Old Trinity Church would be waiting to sing. Even small towns planned parades and speeches.

Driving the Final Spike

On May 8, Leland Stanford arrived in a private train full of honored guests. But

Indians and soldiers watch as workers cheer the joining of the two lines.

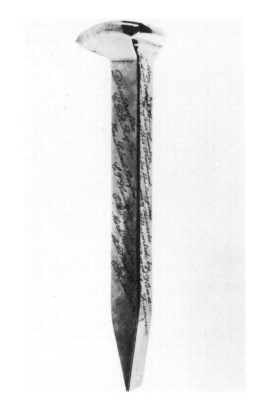

A solid gold spike joined the Union Pacific and Central Pacific railroads.

then Durant wired that his train was held up by a washed-out bridge, and Stanford and the rest of the country had to wait for two days. Durant's train, with General Dodge and General Casement also on board, arrived on May 10.

Under a blue sky, bands played while railroad officials, laborers, Indians, and dance-hall girls gathered around the track. The last crosstie, made of polished California laurel, was laid in place. Then, work crews from both railroads prepared to lay the last two rails. When the rails were finally in place, it was time for the last golden spike, which was placed in its specially prepared hole. Stanford stepped forward, raised the silver-headed hammer high, and swung. He missed. Instead of

hitting the spike, he hit the iron rail. The telegrapher did not wait for another swing. He immediately sent the signal that said, "Done." While the whole country began its postponed celebrations, Stanford stepped back and handed the hammer to Durant, who diplomatically also missed the spike. Then, they shook hands, while the locomotives whistled and the crowds cheered. When the officials stepped back, the locomotive from each railroad advanced until the two were touching. The nation was united.

The very next morning, the first transcontinental train passed through Promontory Point on its way to California. It was only the first of many. From the start, both passenger and freight traffic were heavy. The railroad opened up the West to settlers who came by the millions. As the news of available land spread to Europe, thousands of immigrants arrived to seek a new life. Between 1870 and 1880, the U.S. population grew by twelve million. By 1890, the country west of the Mississippi River had a population of seventeen million.

The railroad also brought prosperity to the West. Cities like Billings, Montana; Cheyenne, Wyoming; and Las Vegas, Nevada, grew up along the line. Industries flourished as a result of newly available natural resources, such as lumber and minerals. Huge cattle ranches spread out across the plains, and every year ranchers drove cattle to the railroad centers. The entire nation gained a supply of fresh beef, and those cattle drives gave birth to the legend of the American cowboy. Factories boomed as laborers worked to supply all the goods needed by the growing population. Agriculture thrived on the prairie and

The final spike is driven into the track at Promontory Point, Utah (above). A herd of Texas longhorns is being driven to a railroad center to be shipped across the country (left).

in California, easily feeding the country's population and creating enough surplus for export. The railroad also promoted an industry called tourism that would eventually bring millions of dollars to the West. Both American and foreign tourists soon discovered the transcontinental railroad after hearing about the West's spectacular scenery and wholesome climate.

Due in large part to the railroads, the United States was booming, and the railroads were becoming the country's first big business. This era was the golden age of railroads.

The Golden Age of Railroads

As soon as the transcontinental railroads were open, branch lines began spreading out on both sides of the tracks. These secondary lines went out from the main line toward small settlements that had grown up around logging camps, mines, and agricultural and cattle centers. Every settlement wanted a railroad line to bring in new residents and supplies and to carry its products to a nationwide market. Those that got a line grew and prospered; those that did not often withered and died. The railroads quickly became the catalyst for prosperity and progress in the West.

At the same time, the railroads continued to grow in the states east of the Mississippi River, especially in the South, where most of the lines had been destroyed during the Civil War. The railroads were one way to unite the country again after the terrible split the war had caused between the North and the South. The railroads spread so rapidly that by 1880, the nation had 93,262 miles of tracks. The biggest period of growth, however, came in the prosperous 1880s, when 70,335 miles of line were laid, bringing the total to 163,597.

From 1865 until 1916, the railroad was king of transportation. The nation was on the move, and the railroad was moving it. But the railroad meant more than transportation to Americans. Wealth and progress were society's main goals during that period, and the railroad symbolized both. As a

result, this period has been called the golden age of railroads.

Tycoons Take Advantage

As the tracks spread out like tentacles on an octopus, the railroads became the first big business in the United States, and the owners became some of the wealthiest and most powerful people in the country. Often, they used that

"Robber barons" such as George Francis Train made millions of dollars through corrupt railroad dealings.

power ruthlessly for their own gain. For a while, there was no one to stop them. After the war, the federal government was too busy trying to heal the nation's wounds to worry about what the new railroad tycoons were doing. Many of them were engaged in corrupt and dishonest activities to kill the competition and make more profit for themselves. Soon, these railroad owners and other unscrupulous industrialists were being called the "robber barons."

One example of corruption involved Thomas Durant of the Union Pacific and a man named George Francis Train. Train was an eccentric millionaire with charm and intelligence. In 1863, Durant and Train saw a way to get rich quickly while building the UP's transcontinental line.

They created a new construction company called the Credit Mobilier of America to build the railway. Since they owned both the railroad and the construction company, they would actually be doing business with themselves. As Credit Mobilier owners, they set inflated prices for construction costs—prices that were outrageously higher than the actual costs. As Union Pacific owners, they paid those high prices to get the railway built. Then, as Credit Mobilier owners again, they pocketed the profit, which was the difference between the actual cost and the inflated prices. Train took his profit and left the railroad business. It became obvious that building a railroad was an easier way to get rich than running one, which is another reason why railroad lines expanded so rapidly in the golden age.

After the transcontinental line was completed in 1869, Durant and the other directors of the Union Pacific began to fight among themselves over control of the company. Durant lost the fight and also lost control of the Credit Mobilier. In his struggle to get it back, the dispute went to the courts and then appeared in the newspaper headlines.

In 1872, the resulting publicity forced Congress to investigate the company, and the scandal that followed rocked the nation. The investigation found that many high government officials, including Vice President Schuyler Colfax, either owned stock in the Credit Mobilier or had accepted bribes from it. It also found that only fifty million of the seventy-three million dollars spent on building the Union Pacific could be justified as actual costs. The owners and stockholders had walked away with twenty-three million dollars. One Credit Mobilier owner was censured, or reprimanded, by Congress, but no one went to jail. Durant himself had already sold his share in the company and spent the remainder of his years in tranquil retirement.

While the robber barons continued to make millions, the people who worked for them often suffered. Work on the railroad was considered romantic, adventurous, and well paying, but it was also tough, dangerous work. Railroad history is full of stories of accidents, collisions, and close calls. One of the strangest involves a worker named "One-Eyed" Jerry Simpson.

Danger Stalks the Railroads

A locomotive hauling lumber up the Cascade Mountains in the Northwest hit a stretch of slippery track and began to slide backward down the mountain. Harvey Reed, the engineer, could not

The job of the brakeman was difficult and dangerous.

locomotive and tender sailed completely over him with room to spare.

Not many workers were as lucky as Simpson. In 1888, the first year accident statistics were gathered, 2,070 railroad workers were killed on the job and 20,148 were injured. As locomotives were improved and made to go faster and faster, more accidents happened. One of the main reasons was the braking system.

At that time, trains had hand brakes, and the controls were positioned on top of each coach. Whenever the engineer whistled the code for a stop, the brakeman had to climb to the roof and run along the top of the swaying, speeding train, stopping on each coach to tighten the brakes. This was difficult enough in warm, dry weather, but many brakemen

control it, so after ordering the fireman to jump, he bailed out and left the train to crash by itself. Meanwhile, back down the mountain a mile, Simpson was sitting on a railroad trestle, or framework, ninety feet above a gorge, hauling up timber. He looked up to see the train racing down the track, heading straight for him. Just before it reached the trestle, the loaded cars broke loose from the locomotive and crashed into the gorge, but the locomotive and tender kept going. There was no time to escape. Knowing he was about to die, Simpson threw himself on the left rail so his death would be quick. The locomotive rushed toward him, swaying back and forth on the rails, as if about to tip over. Just as it reached Simpson, it swayed over to the right, lifting the left wheels completely off the left rail. The

George Westinghouse invented the air brake to improve the safety of train travel.

THE WESTINGHOUSE AIR BRAKE

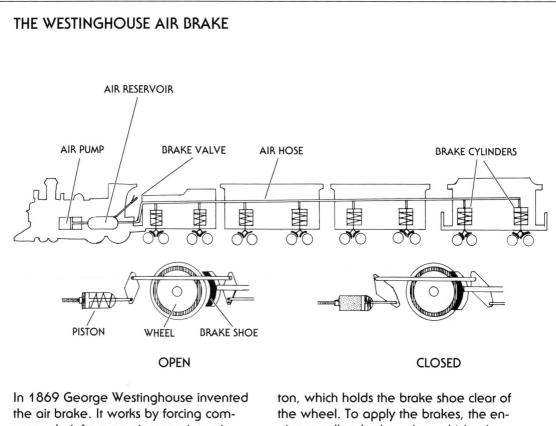

OPEN   CLOSED

In 1869 George Westinghouse invented the air brake. It works by forcing compressed air from an air pump into air hoses connected to brake cylinders positioned alongside the wheels of the locomotive and the other cars. Each brake cylinder contains a piston, which is connected to a brake shoe. The air pressure in the brake cylinder pushes on the piston, which holds the brake shoe clear of the wheel. To apply the brakes, the engineer pulls a brake valve, which releases air from the hoses, creating a vacuum in the brake cylinders. The vacuum pulls the pistons forward, which causes the brake shoes to press against the wheels and stop the train from moving.

lost their lives trying to stop a train quickly in the snow or during an ice storm. And many head-on collisions occurred because it was impossible for the brakeman to move fast enough.

In upstate New York, a young man named George Westinghouse witnessed one of these collisions. He became fascinated by the railroad's braking problem, and by the age of twenty-two, in 1869, he had invented the solution—the air brake. It allowed the engineer himself to set or release every brake on the entire train at the same time. By pumping a steady supply of air through hoses into the brake cylinders, the brakes were kept open. To apply the brakes, all the engineer had to do was stop the flow of air to the cylinders.

The railroad owners, however, were more interested in making money than in providing safety for workers and passengers, and the new brakes would have cost a great deal to install on all

Railroad workers set fire to a bridge during an 1877 strike against unfair wages and dangerous working conditions.

the locomotives. The brakemen on most railroads continued to set brakes by hand. Indeed, the brakemen likely had the most dangerous duties on the railroad because they also had to couple and uncouple the railroad cars.

Cars were hitched together with a device called a link-and-pin coupler. One half of the coupler, on one car, was a big U-shaped metal link with the closed end of the U facing out. It slid into a metal fixture on the other car, and then a big, metal pin was placed through a hole in the top of the fixture and down through the link. This device accounted for most of the deaths and injuries on the railroad. In order to couple two cars, the brakeman had to stand between them to guide the link into the fixture and then fix the pin. Time after time, the link missed the fixture and cut off the brakeman's fingers or hand instead. Often the two cars crashed, killing or injuring the brakeman.

Looking for a Safe Alternative

In 1868, Eli Janney, a Confederate Army major, invented a coupling device he called a knuckle coupler. The two halves gripped each other automatically, much like a handshake, when the cars were pushed together. The brakemen no longer had to stand between the cars but instead could direct the operation from the side. The railroads also considered Janney's invention too expensive.

Years passed while both Westinghouse and Janney tried unsuccessfully to get their inventions accepted. In 1874, a man named Lorenzo Coffin took up their cause after seeing a brakeman lose two fingers in a coupling accident. For years after that, Coffin worked hard to get air brakes and knuckle couplers put on locomotives. Finally, in 1886, a group

The strike of 1877 resulted in more than one hundred deaths.

called the Master Car Builders agreed to hold public tests of the air brake. With Coffin, Westinghouse, Janney, and many railroad officials present, a locomotive equipped with air brakes and pulling a long, heavy train sped down a steeply sloping track at forty miles an hour. At a given signal, the engineer applied the air brakes, and the train stopped smoothly within five hundred feet. Safety concerns eventually won out. By 1888, Coffin had written the first national railroad safety appliance law, requiring air brakes and automatic couplers on all trains. On

Strikers force a brakeman and an engineer from a train during 1877's labor unrest.

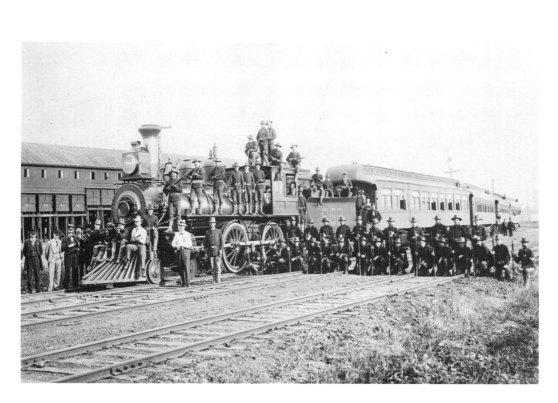

(top) The government called on state militias and the army to end railroad strikes.
(bottom) Traveling salesman George Pullman invented the sleeping car to improve the comfort of train travel.

March 2, 1893, almost a quarter of a century after the inventions had been patented, the law went into effect.

In the meantime, the railroads maintained safety precautions and efficiency in their operations by imposing an almost military discipline on their workers. Rigid work schedules and rules were strictly enforced. Although workers found some of those rules not in their best interest, it was years before they formed unions to fight them. The first union, the Brotherhood of Locomotive Engineers, was formed in 1863 strictly as a social and mutual-aid society. Conductors, firemen, and brakemen also formed unions by 1883, but few workers belonged to these organizations before 1890. Still, when workers had a reason, they did unite against their employers.

In July 1877, a workers' strike had disastrous consequences. Between 1873 and 1877, the Baltimore & Ohio Railroad (B&O) twice cut workers' wages by 10 percent. Finally, the brakemen and firemen, aware of the corruption and the millions being made by the owners, walked off the job. Strikers attacked B&O property in Baltimore and Pittsburgh. In Pittsburgh alone, the damaged property was worth five million dollars. As the strike and violence spread throughout the East and as far west as Chicago, the police, the state militia, and the regular army were called out to stop it. When it was over, one hundred people had been killed and five hundred wounded. The strike had failed. In fact, most early strikes failed because the unions were not organized and because the government stood behind the railroads—and their money. But the day would come when railroad workers would have some of the strongest and most successful unions in the country.

Passengers Ride in Luxury

Although railroad workers had reason to complain about conditions on the

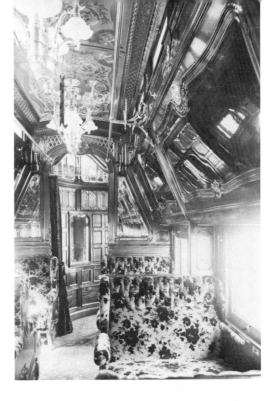

Some of Pullman's sleeping cars were plush and ornate.

railroad, most passengers did not. By this time, George Pullman had introduced luxury train travel. Pullman, born in 1831, was a traveling salesman for a while in the late 1840s when overnight travel on trains was exhausting and

Pullman built the first model sleeping car in 1859.

CHAPTER 5 ■ 57

uncomfortable. He started thinking about sleeping cars, and in 1859, when he had accumulated some money, he decided to build a model. After persuading the Chicago, Alton & St. Louis Railroad to lend him two day coaches, he remodeled the cars into sleepers. During the day, the passengers sat in richly upholstered seats, and at night, the seat backs folded down to form beds for which a mattress and one blanket were provided. The car also had one community washbasin. Perhaps Pullman's most innovative idea was to include a conductor whose sole job was to make up the bunks and serve the passengers. Later, Pullman conductors were to earn fame for their efficiency and service, but the first ones had a hard time just persuading passengers to take their boots off before they went to bed.

Pullman's fledgling enterprise was cut short when the Civil War started, but in 1864, he invested $20,170 to build an all-new sleeping car he called the *Pioneer*. The fact that most passenger cars then cost only $4,000 reveals how luxurious the *Pioneer* was. The interior gleamed with polished black walnut, ornate candle chandeliers, and solid marble washstands. Linen sheets were provided for the beds. Not only did the comfortable seats recline into bottom bunks, but hinged upper bunks were folded up against the ceiling. Unfortunately, in order to fit in all this luxury, Pullman had to make his car wider and higher than any other car in the United States. It was too wide for some

Some trains offered amenities such as barber salons, libraries with organs, and restaurant-quality food.

Massive, grand, and ornate stations became symbols of a railroad's wealth.

station platforms and too high for some overpasses, and no railroad would go to the expense of altering its tracks to accommodate the car. The *Pioneer* became known as "Pullman's Folly."

But the *Pioneer* soon gained acceptance despite these problems. When President Lincoln was assassinated, his home state of Illinois asked the Chicago & Alton to include the *Pioneer* in his funeral train. The railroad was forced to alter the platforms and overpasses, and thousands of people saw Pullman's car.

The publicity brought success, and in 1867, Pullman formed the Pullman Palace Car Company and operated forty-eight cars. That same year, he built his first "hotel" car, the *President*, a sleeper car equipped with a kitchen. Passengers were served meals at small tables set up near their seats and had among their choices steak and potatoes for sixty cents or ham for forty cents. This service was such a success that the very next year, Pullman introduced the first dining car, the *Delmonico*.

From then on, railroads competed with each other to offer passengers the most luxury. They provided club cars where men (but not women) could drink and smoke, hairdressing and barber salons, ornate parlor cars with libraries and organs, and observation cars for enjoying the scenery. Dining cars offered menus that could compete with the best restaurants. Steam heat and electric lights were added in the 1880s.

This trend culminated around the turn of the century with special trains called "limiteds." The most famous of these luxury trains was the *Twentieth Century Limited,* which began service between Chicago and New York City in 1902. For passengers who wished to pay the additional fare, the train offered private bedrooms, bridal suites, full bathrooms, on-board secretarial staff, and bulletins of the lastest stock market prices. And every car was staffed with well-trained Pullman employees who offered service equal to that of the best hotels.

ELECTRIC LOCOMOTIVES

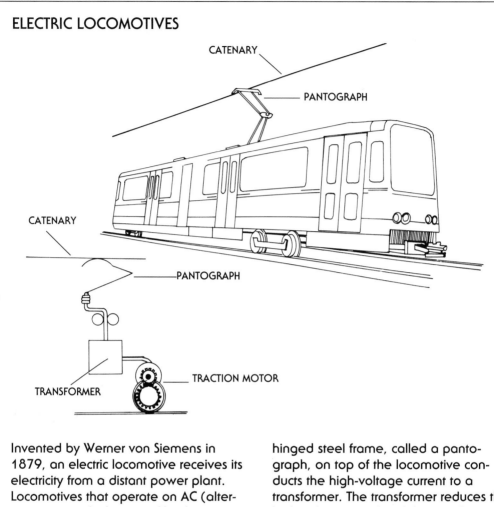

Invented by Werner von Siemens in 1879, an electric locomotive receives its electricity from a distant power plant. Locomotives that operate on AC (alternating current) electricity, like the one shown here, get their power from an overhead wire called a catenary. A hinged steel frame, called a pantograph, on top of the locomotive conducts the high-voltage current to a transformer. The transformer reduces the high voltage to a level that can be used to operate traction motors, which turn the locomotive's drive wheels.

The main railroad stations were also places where the railroad companies could show off their wealth and lure more passengers. As the golden age of railroads progressed, these stations became great halls of stone, glass, and iron, marked by grand architectural features such as columns, canopies, buttresses, and turrets. The many rooms contained offices, restaurants, shops, and hotels.

Stations were the center of railroad life and, in some ways, the center of nineteenth-century life. In villages and cities, railroad stations were where people met and socialized, where news and gossip were exchanged, where books and newspapers were sold, and where food and other goods were delivered. A city station was a scene of frenzied activity at any hour, but the crowds before and after work in New York, Chicago,

Boston, and other large cities gave birth to the term *rush hour.* Thousands of people jammed the ticket windows, waiting rooms, and platforms. They scurried through corridors and mazes of booths, gates, and doorways. Carts piled high with luggage, mailbags, and packages weaved in and out through the crowds. Steam locomotives hissed and puffed while, still louder, came the announcements of arriving and departing trains. Choking smoke and soot from the coal-fed locomotives permeated the air.

Electricity Offers New Possibilities

The railroads could not do very much about the crowds, but in the 1880s, they discovered there was something they could do about the smoke and soot. A German engineer named Werner von Siemens built and demonstrated an electric locomotive in Berlin in 1879.

Electric locomotives were quiet, nonpolluting, and capable of great speed. Then as now, the electricity that runs these trains is produced externally, in a central power plant, not on board the train.

Locomotives receive the electricity from that power plant in one of two ways: either through an electrified overhead wire called a catenary or from an electrified third rail that runs beside the other two rails on the track. In the catenary system, a hinged steel frame called a pantograph sits on top of the locomotive and connects it to the catenary. The electricity travels from the power plant through the catenary, then through the pantograph and down to motors near the locomotive's wheels. The motors

The exploits of train robber Jesse James (both) became legendary. Frank James joined his brother Jesse in robbing trains.

turn the wheels. In the third-rail system, the locomotive has a metal device called a shoe underneath it. The shoe slides along the third rail and conducts electricity to the motors.

The Baltimore & Ohio built the world's first mainline electric railroad in 1895. Baltimore's city officials were tired of the noise, steam, and soot and ordered the railroad company to stop running steam locomotives through the city. Using the catenary system, the electric locomotives ran through and under Baltimore, towing the trains and their steam locomotives. Electric trains were also the perfect solution to a similar problem in New York's Grand Central Station, where trains approached and departed the platforms through long tunnels that were always terribly polluted. But the New York Central did not want to spend the money to install the new trains. Then, one day in January 1902, smoke in the tunnel was so bad

that it obscured the signals and caused a catastrophic collision. Immediately afterward, a third-rail system was installed.

Several ambitious electrification projects, some on railroads in the Cascade and Rocky mountains, were completed before 1916. Except for trolley and streetcar lines, however, the country did not rush to convert to this new technology. The railroads had a great deal of money tied up in their old equipment and did not want to invest the huge sums needed to replace it. Besides, the country was still in love with steam locomotives, and the fuel to run them was plentiful and cheap.

Reaching into Popular Culture

Public admiration of the railroads was evident everywhere in the culture. On Broadway, popular hits were *The Fast*

Engineer Casey Jones, seated in the cab, became the heroic subject of a famous ballad after he died in a train collision.

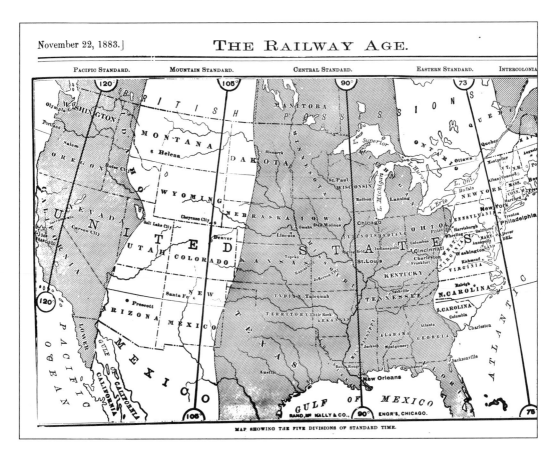

PACIFIC STANDARD.   MOUNTAIN STANDARD.   CENTRAL STANDARD.   EASTERN STANDARD.   INTERCOLONIA

MAP SHOWING THE FIVE DIVISIONS OF STANDARD TIME.

To operate on schedule, railroads instituted four standard time zones in 1883.

Mail and *The Ninety and Nine,* both plays about the railroad. In 1903, the movies appeared, and the first screen classic was entitled *The Great Train Robbery.* The real train robberies began in 1866 and were a constant threat to the railroads for fifty years, but the daring escapades of some of the robbers made them legends. Jesse James and his brother Frank, Sam Bass, and Butch Cassidy and the Sundance Kid were some of the men who captured the public's imagination. The railroad was so popular that even honest railroad workers became legends. Railroad engineer John Luther Jones came from Cayce, Kentucky, so his friends called him Casey. On April 30, 1900, he died, some say heroically, at the throttle of his locomotive, trying to stop a collision. After his death, a coworker named Walace Saunders composed a ballad about him that began:

> Come all you rounders, I want you to hear
> The story told of a brave engineer.
> Old Casey Jones was the rounder's name;
> On a six-eight wheeler he won his fame.

The ballad caught on with the public, and Casey Jones is still perhaps the country's most famous railroad engineer.

Americans read about these legends in magazines and dime novels. They could even read stories of famous writers from abroad. Charles Dickens, for example, published popular railroad stories, but he may have felt that the love for railroads had gone a bit far when he wrote: "There were railway hotels, coffee-houses, lodging-houses, boarding-houses; railway plans, maps, views, wrappers, bottles, sandwich-boxes and timetables; railway hackney-coach and cabstands; railway omnibuses, railway streets and buildings, railway hangers-on and parasites, and flatterers out of all calculation. There was even railway time observed in clocks, as if the sun itself had given in."

Dickens's mention of "railway time" refers to a railroad innovation that changed forever the way Americans thought about time. Since sunrise and sunset varied across the nation, there were many different local times. Michigan, for instance, had twenty-seven local times; Wisconsin had thirty-eight. This variance made it almost impossible for the railroads to operate on a timetable. So railroad officials held a conference and decided to divide the country into four time zones—Eastern, Central, Mountain, and Pacific, each varying in time by an hour. At noon on November 18, 1883, the new system went into effect across the nation.

Many people objected, saying they would rather live by God's time than the railroad's. And many people ignored it and missed their trains. But, on the whole, the change went smoothly. When Congress finally passed the Standard Time Act, which defined the boundaries of each zone, on March 18, 1918, the United States had already been operating on the railroad's standard time for thirty-five years.

Developing a Modern Nation

The golden age of railroads changed more than the country's time. It changed the nature of American society. By 1916, the United States was no longer a young, struggling nation made up of isolated settlements and wilderness. It was a mature nation full of prosperous farms and bustling cities. The people no longer identified themselves primarily as Chicagoans, Southerners, Irish, or Chinese but as Americans.

The nation was wealthy. The railroad had spread the Industrial Revolution rapidly throughout the country and had strengthened commerce and industry by creating an ever-growing market for its goods and services. The United States was becoming an economic leader in the world. As the country's first big business, the railroads had helped create a modern economy based on commerce and trade rather than agriculture. It had developed an efficient way to run big business that served as an example to the many other forms of business that followed. Railroads created new careers and provided jobs for almost two million people. In fact, by 1916, one of every twenty-five workers was employed by the railroads.

And the United States was strong and united. On the eve of World War I in 1916, Americans did not doubt that they could defend their nation, if necessary. But it was not the nation that would have to defend its territory in the coming years. It was the railroads. The golden age of railroads was ending.

Decline of American Railroads

When the golden age peaked in the United States in 1916, more than 1,300 railroads were operating on a total of 254,000 miles of track. By 1960, there were only 660 railroads operating on 220,000 miles of track. Those companies that were left were no longer either rich or powerful. They were struggling to survive.

The decline of the railroads was caused by two major forces: government regulation and competition from new forms of transportation. Those forces would almost destroy the passenger service and would reduce railroad freight traffic from 77 percent of the nation's total in 1916 to 35 percent in 1980. The railroads themselves, however, are to blame for the early problems that started the decline. The power, greed, and corruption of many railroad owners caused these problems.

Railroad companies in the golden age had a monopoly on the business. This meant they had no competition and could run the railroads as they pleased. These companies thought no one had the right to interfere with their actions. One portion of the public disagreed.

The freight shippers, who were the customers paying the railroad to carry their produce and goods to the markets, were angered by the corruption and decided to fight back. The rates the railroads charged were not based on the weight of a shipment or on how many miles it had to go; instead, the rates were based on what the railroad thought the service was worth. Shippers thought this was unfair, and the practice led to rate discrimination, which means that the railroads charged different shippers different rates for the same freight. In 1885, for example, it was discovered that an Ohio railroad was charging John D. Rockefeller's Standard Oil Company ten cents a barrel for shipping oil but was charging smaller oil companies thirty-five cents a barrel

Railroad companies gave rebates to Standard Oil owner John D. Rockefeller so that he would continue to use their services.

President Woodrow Wilson nationalized the railroads during World War I.

it at the time, these regulations were the first step in the decline of the railroads.

Railroad lawyers fought these laws all the way to the Supreme Court but had no success until 1886, when the Supreme Court ruled that states could not regulate any rates on goods going outside their borders. It was time for the federal government to act. In 1887, Congress created the Interstate Commerce Commission (ICC) to regulate rates and guarantee equal treatment to all shippers. Although the ICC did not really have much power, it set a precedent for federal regulation, which contributed to the railroads' decline.

In the years that followed, distrust of the railroads continued to grow, even though the railroad owners were more limited in power. Between 1890 and 1913, the federal government passed several more acts that increased the ICC's power and took away the railroads' ability to raise rates to increase their income. The railroads needed more income because they were investing in improvements. At the same time, workers' unions began demanding higher wages. Furthermore, between 1900 and 1915, the railroads' tax bills tripled while their income only doubled. The railroads had begun to feel a financial pinch by the time the United States entered World War I in April 1917.

on the same route. The railroad was giving the twenty-five-cent difference to Standard Oil as a rebate. In other words, the company was bribing Standard Oil to continue using its service because Standard Oil was a large client that would bring lots of business.

Rate discrimination and rebates were not illegal at the time, but the shippers decided they should be. The independent, strong-willed wheat farmers of the Midwest were especially outraged. Those farmers, called Grangers, belonged to an association called the National Grange of the Patrons of Husbandry. Its large membership used its political influence between 1871 and 1874 to persuade the states of Illinois, Wisconsin, Minnesota, and Iowa to pass laws regulating railroad freight rates. Although no one realized

Putting the Railroads Under Government Control

The war put huge demands on all the country's resources but particularly on the railroads, which were essentially the only means of transporting war materials and troops. Partly because they were angry at the government and partly because regulation had hampered their ability to respond, the railroads did not meet demands quickly enough to please the government. As a result, President Woodrow Wilson nationalized the railroads—that is, put them under government control—on December 28, 1917, and appointed U.S. Treasury Secretary William McAdoo as the director. This, too, contributed to the decline of the railroads.

In some ways, McAdoo made the railroads more efficient. He eliminated duplicate trains and stations, coordinated competing routes, and bought 2,000 new locomotives and 100,000 new cars. But he did not repair damage done to tracks and equipment by the wear and tear of the war effort, and he raised workers' wages a number of times. By the time the government gave the railroads back to their owners in 1920, fifty-five cents of every dollar the railroad earned went to pay the workers. The railroad used 94.3 percent of its income to pay for all expenses.

Some people wanted the railroads to remain under government control after the war, but this idea did not receive much support. Instead, Congress passed another act increasing the power and responsibilities of the ICC. For instance, the railroads now had to have the ICC's permission to merge, to build new lines, and to abandon old ones.

This act was the biggest step in the decline of the railroads so far, because it decreased the railroads' ability to compete at a time when they faced increasing competition from new forms of transportation. Pipelines were being

William McAdoo increased the railroads' efficiency but decreased their profits.

built to carry gas and oil, buses were carrying passengers, trucks were carrying freight on short hauls, and fledgling airlines were appearing. Plus, there was the automobile. The American public had discovered cars, which were rapidly becoming more popular than trains.

The railroads fought back in the 1920s. They continued to develop new technology and introduced faster, more efficient locomotives, which allowed them to carry more freight. They repaired tracks with improved rails to accommodate the faster trains. In order to keep their long-distance passengers, the companies concentrated on providing luxury. The *Twentieth Century Limited* now laid out a 6-foot-wide, 260-foot-long red carpet at its departing platform in

The Great Depression quickened the decline of the railroads, as fewer and fewer people could afford to travel.

Grand Central Station in New York City. It also had roomettes, private compartments that were sitting rooms by day and bedrooms by night.

Downhill Slide

In October 1929, when the Great Depression hit the nation, the railroads were in good shape physically, but they were in no shape financially to face the terrible years that lay ahead. The depression turned their slow decline into a fast, downhill slide. The railroads' combined income of $977 million in 1929 became a loss of $122 million in 1932. The labor force dropped by almost 500,000, and the workers who were not laid off took salary cuts. The railroads cut payments to stockholders by 75 percent. They put half the country's locomotives in storage because they could not afford to repair them.

Nothing worked. By 1938, one-third of the nation's approximately 234,000 miles of railroad track was owned by bankrupt companies.

Those tracks were no longer a proud symbol of the king of transportation. Public opinion had changed. It was another sign of the railroads' decline. Now, tracks were seen as dangerous, especially at crossings, where too many automobiles were getting hit by speeding trains. The rights of way were fenced off and were mysterious, almost sinister places containing "jungles," the camps of train-hopping hoboes made jobless and homeless by the depression. In many cities, slums grew up around the stations, as the upper classes moved farther out to the suburbs. No one went to the stations except passengers. In towns, someone who was poor was said to live "on the wrong side of the tracks." With their public image at an all-time low, the railroads needed to do something to woo the public back. It was a matter of survival. So, in the midst of the Great Depression, while some companies were going broke, other railroads developed and introduced an exciting new type of locomotive called the diesel.

Innovation Captures Imagination

Diesels, named after their German inventor, Rudolf Diesel, are actually electric locomotives that produce their own power. The diesel engine in the locomotive works by using pistons to compress, or squeeze, the air inside cylinders. Most engines have from twelve to sixteen cylinders. When the air is compressed, it heats up. This heat sets fire to diesel oil fuel that is injected into the cylinder. The fired fuel produces power to drive a machine called a generator, which, in turn, produces electricity. Motors use the electricity to turn the locomotive's wheels.

When the first diesel in the United States began moving trains around a New York City railroad yard in 1925, everyone could see that it was quieter, cleaner, and more efficient than steam locomotives. But no one realized that diesels would replace steam locomotives completely by 1960. In 1934, the first diesel-powered passenger train, the *Pioneer Zephyr*, went from Denver to Chicago in just over thirteen hours at an average speed of 77.6 miles per hour. The public was enthralled. It was not just the speed or the luxurious accommodations or even the air-conditioning

Quicker, more efficient diesel locomotives rekindled the public's interest in train travel.

THE DIESEL-ELECTRIC ENGINE

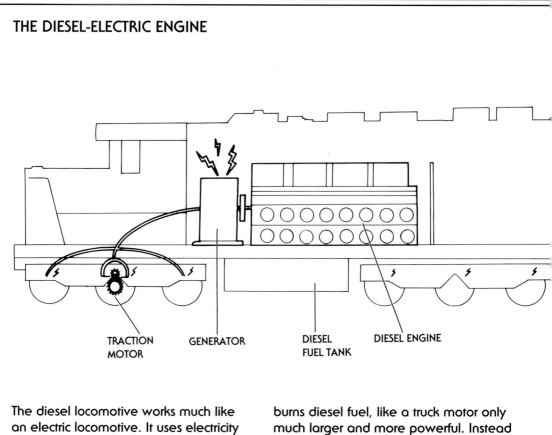

TRACTION
MOTOR GENERATOR DIESEL
FUEL TANK DIESEL ENGINE

The diesel locomotive works much like an electric locomotive. It uses electricity to drive traction motors that propel the locomotive. But instead of getting its electricity from a distant source, the diesel produces its own electricity. This is done with a combustion motor that burns diesel fuel, like a truck motor only much larger and more powerful. Instead of being used to turn a transmission, however, as it would on a truck, this diesel motor turns the turbine of a generator, which produces the electricity for the traction motors.

but the design that captured their imagination. The diesel was streamlined, with smooth, round curves to reduce air resistance. It was sleek, modern, and shiny silver. These streamliners, as they came to be called, symbolized the hope for a bright, prosperous future made possible by new technology. Soon, every railroad that could afford it was running streamlined trains, and their popularity was gaining back some of the lost passengers.

It cost more to buy diesel locomotives than steam locomotives, but in the end, they saved the railroad money. They cost less to run, needed less maintenance, could go one thousand miles without servicing, and did less damage to the tracks because of their lighter weight. They were also easier to run, and unlike steam locomotives that had to build up a head of steam before they could run, diesels turned on and off on demand. By 1941, diesels were also being used for freight trains. Freight traffic began to pick up in 1939 after war again broke out in Europe. The United States was rearming for the fight. The heavier traffic in coal, steel, oil, and related products increased railroad profits by 25 percent in 1941.

Fleeting Prosperity

After the United States entered World War II in December 1941, the railroads enjoyed their greatest prosperity since before 1917. Determined not to be nationalized again, they cooperated fully with the federal government. With one-third fewer employees, cars, and locomotives than they had in 1918, they moved 50 percent more freight each year. They transported 90 percent of the military traffic, and that included delivering one billion barrels of oil to the East Coast every day. At the same time, passengers returned to the railroad in droves because they were unable to get gasoline and tires for their cars. Day and night, fully loaded trains rolled across the country. Before the war was over in 1945, the railroads were taking in record profits, and a number of railroads were out of bankruptcy. Instead of costing the taxpayers two million dollars a day as the nationalized railroads had in World War I, the railroads paid three million dollars a day in taxes.

Unfortunately, the prosperity did not last once the war was over. Rolling stock and tracks were nearly worn out

The sleek lines of the diesel streamliners attracted travelers.

After World War II, trains could not compete with the public's infatuation with the automobile.

from the hard use, and the railroads had to spend billions to replace them.

As diesel power continued to replace steam, labor problems arose. One of the ways diesels saved the railroads money was by eliminating labor. For instance, firemen were needed in steam locomotives to feed fuel to the engine, but diesels did not need to be fed. For years, the railroads fought government regulations and labor unions for the right to stop using firemen on trains. Not until 1964 did they earn the right not to hire any new firemen for freight diesels, although those already on the job were to be allowed to work until retirement.

There were two main reasons for this battle between railroads and government, a battle that symbolizes the difficulties the railroads faced in the middle of the twentieth century. One is that, with the help of the government, the railroad labor unions opposed changes with such success that railroad labor costs remained among the highest of any industry in the country. The other reason is that the government regulations that made changes in the railroad industry so difficult were based on nineteenth-century thinking. The government wanted the railroads to survive, but also wanted to protect the public from dangers brought about by the railroads' power. That power and its dangers, however, had disappeared before 1920, and the regulations had become a danger to the railroads.

Despite their mighty efforts during World War II, the railroads still did not receive much assistance from the government. And to make matters worse, the government began to subsidize the railroads' competitors, as they had subsidized the railroads in their infancy.

Cars and Jets Dethrone the King

After 1945, the public again began buying automobiles, which had not been available during the war. As the number of cars grew, the public realized how inadequate the nation's roads were and began clamoring for new highways. The government responded by subsidizing the interstate highway system. By the early 1950s, the highways had virtually killed the railroads' short, local passenger services. Since the highways also benefited trucks, the railroads lost much of their freight traffic at the same time.

Again, the railroads fought back. In an effort to save long-distance passenger service, they offered new, luxury supertrains and innovations such as the Vista-Dome, a glass-topped observation car. For a time, this seemed to work, but then, in 1952, the United States entered the jet age with the introduction of jet airline travel. The government began to subsidize airports as well. This competition was too much for the railroads. Americans fell in love with jets, and trains seemed old-fashioned. In order to save money and survive, the railroads had to cut back service and discontinue some trains. Train travel ceased to be either luxurious or convenient, and even people who loved the railroad used it less and less. Fortunately for the railroads, the fight for freight traffic was somewhat more successful. By developing new, specialized rolling stock, they were able to increase some types of freight service. Still, in 1955, the railroads were carrying less than half of the nation's freight traffic.

In 1967, the government delivered the last blow to passenger service by withdrawing its profitable mail service from the trains and giving it to truck companies and airlines. Even the railroads that had been willing to lose money to continue running passenger trains could now no longer afford it. Soon, there were barely five hundred long-distance passenger trains daily as opposed to the fifteen thousand there had been in the late 1930s. Bankruptcies were almost a daily event. It was obvious that passenger trains were not going to survive without government help.

The railroads were forced to compete with trucks for freight service.

Railroads installed Vista-Dome observation cars to attract passengers.

In 1969, the Association of American Railroads petitioned the federal government to subsidize the remaining passenger trains. The government, after helping to push them to the point of ruin, agreed to rescue them at the taxpayers' expense. In 1970, Congress passed an act that created the National Railroad Passenger Corporation (Amtrak). It went into business on April 30, 1971. The act not only provided for federal, state, and local subsidies but also gave the railroads permission to drop their long-distance passenger service if they turned their best passenger cars over to Amtrak. All but three railroads jumped at the chance.

Difficulty Keeping Up

The two hundred passenger trains Amtrak inherited were old and outdated, so they were always late. Because trains were understaffed, they were also dirty. People joked that trains had gotten a bad name: Amtrak. And they called some of the stations "Amshacks." In San Antonio, Texas, passengers detrained into a weed patch. But when new and rebuilt equipment was introduced in the early 1980s, Amtrak's performance improved.

Amtrak now provides passenger service throughout the country, running twenty-four hundred cars along twenty-four thousand miles of track in forty-three states. More than half its business is in the crowded Northeast. There, electric metroliners, which can travel 125 miles per hour but normally go about 90, are so popular that passengers often have to stand. But reservations for sleeping cars on the long-distance routes in the West are also sold out months in advance, even though there are no luxury services. In fact, Amtrak still does not have enough

Amtrak does not have enough equipment to keep up with the nation's increased demand for passenger travel service.

equipment to keep up with the increasing demand for passenger travel, even though it ordered new locomotives and passengers cars worth $150 million in 1990.

In 1984, Amtrak earned $759 million and received $716 million in federal subsidies. By 1988, income had risen to more than $1 billion, and subsidies had been reduced to $581 million. Despite this decreasing dependence on the government, most experts think subsidies will always be required. And they point out that this is only fair, since the government is also still subsidizing airports and highways. Even with the subsidies, however, Amtrak cannot afford the improvements to tracks and equipment that would allow it to take advantage of new high-speed technology.

The late 1960s were also bad years for the freight railroads. In 1968, the railroad world was shocked by the merger of two old enemies, the New York Central and the Pennsylvania Railroad. Between them, they handled most of the freight traffic in the Northeast. The merger, however, was a disaster. The new Penn Central could not make enough income to survive. It blamed its failure on having to pay "too many workers to run too many empty cars over too many miles of worn track on which it paid too many taxes." By 1974, the Northeast, which contained much of the country's industry, needed transportation alternatives and was about to lose its railroads. Again, the federal government came to the rescue.

The government formed the Consolidated Rail Corporation (Conrail) to take over all the failing Northeast freight lines. Starting on April 1, 1976, with $7 million in government money, aging equipment, 24,000 miles of deteriorating track, and 90,000 employees, Conrail was expected to be self-sufficient within four

President Jimmy Carter partially deregulated the railroads.

Conrail has been operating with fair success under private ownership.

Whatever success Conrail and the other railroads have had in the 1980s is partly due to the Staggers Rail Act signed into law by President Jimmy Carter on October 14, 1980. After a century of strict government regulation, the railroads were finally partially deregulated. They can now set their own rates without ICC approval. The ICC, however, still has authority over mergers.

A Quiet Revolution

Deregulation set a quiet railroad revolution in motion. During the 1980s, there were more giant mergers. The railroads eliminated miles of underused track and pared down their fleets of rolling stock. Managers sought new technologies to improve their railroads and new marketing techniques to sell them to the shippers.

or five years. The government was willing to continue subsidizing passenger traffic for the public good but felt that freight railroads should remain private business. By 1981, Conrail had used more than $3.3 billion of the government's money. It had, however, made a small profit for the first time. By March 1987, when the government put Conrail on the market for sale, it had pared its track down to 11,900 miles, its employees to 35,500, and had an income of more than $400 million. Since then,

Perhaps the most interesting move in the revolution is the attempt to revive small railroads. Entrepreneurs are buying or leasing lines abandoned by the big railroads and some of these lines are making a profit. This revolution is so new, no one knows what the outcome will be. Despite some promising trends, American railroads are still very troubled, and no one has an easy solution. But in most other developed countries in the world, it is quite a different story.

Worldwide Success and the Future

While the railroads struggle to survive in the United States, they are thriving in the other developed nations of the world, where fast trains travel regularly between major cities and provide dependable, convenient service. New technology is frequently introduced to make train service even better. Because of this, many people have always used the railroads regularly. The trains have remained an integral part of the total transportation system in many countries.

There are several reasons for this success, but the main reason is quite simple: the railroads are owned and operated by the national governments. Most of the world's railroads make little or no profit, and they do not have to because the government supports them. When the companies want to research and develop new technology, the government pays for it. When it comes time to build the technologically advanced trains, the government covers the expenses. With this kind of backing, foreign railroads have never had to worry about failure.

Nevertheless, these railroads have also made some wise decisions through the years and have been very responsive to issues as they arose. For instance, Italy, France, and Switzerland realized early in this century that electricity was the cleanest, cheapest, and fastest mode of operation. Despite the higher initial building cost, they concentrated on building electric lines and locomotives, which later put them ahead in the race for high-speed technology.

Giving People What They Want

After the railroads in Europe and Great Britain were almost destroyed during World War II, rebuilding them was an expensive burden. But most countries took the opportunity to modernize their lines, primarily with electricity.

The exception was Great Britain. Like the United States, it converted instead to diesel power. The main reason was lack of funding. The European nations received vast amounts of financial aid from the United States after the war, but Great Britain did not. It was not until the mid-1950s that Great Britain could afford to think about modernizing its railroads. Previously, the country had invested heavily in diesel engines to keep its railroads running. Replacing them seemed a foolish expense, especially since oil to run the diesels was then so cheap and plentiful. Moreover, the oil companies were acquiring a great deal of power, as they were in the United States, and they used that power to fight the conversion to electricity.

They wanted the railroads to run diesels that used oil.

In the 1950s, the world's railroads faced the same increasing competition from highway and air traffic as the railroads in the United States did, but their response was more successful. Geography played a part. Most developed nations are quite small. It takes much less money and time to build, maintain, and operate railroads in a country the size of France or Japan than it does in a country as big as the United States. Also, their urban centers are closer together. Often, it is just as fast or faster to take the train between cities as it is to fly. It is also true that automobiles, gas, and airfares have always been more expensive in Europe than in the United States. In many cases, it was simply more economical for people to take the train. Nevertheless, the railroads had to fight for their share of the traffic, and they won.

Their main strategy was a simple one: find out what people want and give it to them. The best example of this is the Trans-Europe Express (TEE), a concept dreamed up by Dutch Railways president F. Q. den Hollander in the early 1950s. He realized that as prosperity returned to Europe after the war, businesspeople were traveling more and wanted to be able to go out, do their business, and return home in the same day. His goal was to make this possible by train on an international basis. The luxurious trains he envisioned would be first-class-only express trains, meaning they would stop only at the main stations of major cities. He faced quite a task.

Europeans Forge Ahead

First, Hollander had to convince France, West Germany, Luxembourg, the Netherlands, Switzerland, and Italy to join. Since planes could fly over international borders without stopping, he had to assure that the trains would also be able to speed from country to country. He persuaded the border authorities of all the countries to conduct customs and passport checks on board the train while it

Train travel is much more popular in Europe than in America.

Japanese high-speed trains can travel as fast as 160 miles per hour.

traveled at normal speed. But his next step was not so successful.

Hollander wanted to offer a network of standardized trains running on coordinated schedules. Timing the schedules was possible, but the countries could not agree on a standard design for the trains. Every country wanted to use the trains it already had. When the TEE opened in 1957, four different types of diesel trains were in use. The only thing standard about them was air-conditioning and an exterior that was painted red and cream. Electric trains were added to the TEE gradually as more and more lines were electrified and new technology eliminated electricity incompatibilities among the various countries. For twenty years, the TEE competed successfully with the airlines. But in the late 1970s, the airlines began offering more flights and aggressively

marketing them. At the same time, the member countries began to concentrate more heavily on their own rail services. By the 1980s, the TEE had been reduced to a few special cars tacked on to other express trains at rush hours.

In its time, the TEE contributed two invaluable services to European railroads. First, it offered strong competition to the airlines at a critical time. Second, as countries competed to contribute better trains, the TEE spurred the development of new technology. Much of that development was concentrated on making trains go faster. Studies showed that every 1 percent rise in train speed was matched by a 1 percent rise in passenger travel. The French set the pace. They began a research program in the mid-1950s to explore the outer limits of speed for a flanged wheel on a steel rail. Although

A bullet train travels on elevated tracks through downtown Tokyo.

one of their trains reached 205.6 miles per hour on a straight, twenty-five-mile stretch of track in 1955, it would be a quarter of a century before they could build a train that could handle high speed on a daily basis without breaking down frequently or costing too much to maintain.

Japanese Go High-Speed

In the meantime, the Japanese National Railroad beat them to it. In 1964, it opened the New Tokaido Line between Tokyo and Osaka, the first of the *shinkansen*, which means "new railways" in Japanese. Most other countries call them bullet trains because of the shape of their noses. The electric *shinkansen* flash through Japan at 125 miles per hour, although they are capable of going 160. They are fully automated and are oper-

ated remotely from a control center in one of the two terminal cities. The engineer goes along for the ride.

The *shinkansen* immediately set records for performance, passenger service, and economy that amazed the world and delighted the Japanese. Within a few years, more than eighty trains a day were running each way, and on one day in 1969, more than half a million passengers traveled on the line. Even the average number of daily passengers seems incredible: a quarter of a million. The only major complaint about the *shinkansen* is that they are noisy. In urban areas, where the trains roll right by houses and office buildings, the railroad has had to erect sound barriers on either side of the track. But, on the whole, the trains are a success, and the Japanese have continued to build new *shinkansen* throughout their country.

(top) The French TGV, or high-speed trains, are the fastest and most successful trains in the world.
(bottom) This French TGV traveled 322 miles per hour to break the world rail speed record.

In 1964, when the *shinkansen* started service, the French National Railroad was just deciding to build a high-speed line to ease the crowded traffic on the regular line from Paris to Lyons, a distance of 317 miles (507 kilometers). It took fourteen more years to build the electrified track and the trains. The trains are officially called TGV for *train a grande vitesse,* meaning "high-speed train" in French. But the French people have affectionately nicknamed the TGV the *Oranges* for their color.

When the first TGV was tested in 1978, it reached a speed of 236 miles per hour, a world record. For passenger use, however, the top speed is generally kept to about 186 miles per hour. When the trains went into regular service in September 1981, they were an instant success. The airlines had to cut their flights on the Paris-to-Lyons route in half. The TGV is still considered the most successful train in the world, and more lines are being built in France.

Constructing these lines is a slow process because they are difficult to build. High-speed trains require special tracks. They must be absolutely flat, smooth, and straight. The tracks must also be dedicated, or reserved for the

high-speed train only, because it would be too difficult and unsafe to schedule its runs around the runs of slower trains. Moreover, heavier, older trains would ruin the special tracks.

Most high-speed lines are built in densely populated areas, and building a straight line through those areas means displacing many people, businesses, and buildings to clear the path. Since they must be absolutely flat, the lines require many bridges, overpasses, and tunnels. These difficulties make the lines very expensive to build. The 317 miles of the first TGV line cost the French $1.5 billion. That is the main reason TGVs are not now speeding passengers to their destinations all over the world. For many railroads, including those in the United States and even many nationalized railroads, the cost has simply been too great. But, despite the cost, the situation is about to change.

High-Speed Links

In 1992, Great Britain and part of Europe are set to become joined economically into the European Community (EC). This is a joint venture among twelve coun-

tries to harmonize trade and economic policies in the hope of greater prosperity. The railroads in those countries have decided to play a big role. If they succeed, they could usher in a new railroad age.

The railroads' plan, which has its roots in the old TEE, includes a network of high-speed trains connecting major cities in the twelve EC countries as well as Austria and Switzerland. It will require building forty-six hundred miles of track and upgrading twelve thousand more by 2015 to accommodate trains traveling between 120 and 200 miles per hour. The estimated cost is a staggering $100 billion. The plan includes a high-speed rail link between London and Europe via the tunnel being built under the English Channel, which connects Dover, England, and Calais, France. The Channel Tunnel is due to be completed for both rail and road traffic in 1993, although England does not anticipate finishing the high-speed track between London and Dover until 1998. Until then, conventional trains will carry passengers between London and Calais.

By 1993, however, high-speed trains are scheduled to carry passengers from Calais to Paris and to Brussels, Belgium. Links may also be available by then to

As part of the plan to unite Europe's rail systems, a high-speed track will be built in the tunnel beneath the English Channel. High-speed trains, such as this model, will carry passengers between Dover, England and Calais, France.

Germany and Spain. When the high-speed network throughout Europe is completed, people will be able to have breakfast in the Netherlands, lunch in France, and dinner in Italy without leaving the ground. Countries on the edges of Europe, such as Portugal and Greece, would likely develop closer ties to the rest of Europe. Recent changes in the Soviet Union could lead to other countries joining the high-speed rail network someday, providing a valuable link between East and West.

Total success, however, is not assured. There is public opposition in some countries and technology must still be worked out. Many countries will have difficulty financing their share of the network. Regardless of whether the plan succeeds totally or partially, it shows that Europe has faith in the railroads and in their future.

Workers carve out a tunnel beneath the English Channel. Europeans hope to complete the Channel Tunnel by 1993.

America's airports have become increasingly congested. High-speed trains would reduce this congestion and provide an alternative for travelers.

Regaining Ground

Only thirty years ago, when jet travel was new, many people were saying that the railroads would not survive. But now it seems that railroads will be an integral part of the future of transportation. The United States is the only major industrialized nation where there is still any serious debate over the future of rail-passenger service, and even here, railroad promoters are gaining ground. Many things have happened in the last thirty years to change their minds.

Airline travel itself has contributed to that change. While it is still the fastest way to travel long distances, it is not always the most convenient. Airports are often located at some distance from the cities. Because of traffic congestion on the highways, the trip to the airport sometimes takes longer than the flight itself. At the busier airports, runways are also congested, and planes may have to wait in line to take off and land. Many people would gladly take high-speed trains to avoid this congestion.

Competition among the airlines, plus the high price of fuel, have driven many airlines into bankruptcy. Surviving airlines have had to raise their rates and cut back on both the number of flights and the number of cities served. Many people are finding they cannot travel to their destination by plane. The gaps left by those canceled routes are perfect for high-speed trains to take over.

Automobile travel has also become less attractive, as crowded highways, air pollution, and high gas prices become major concerns in urban areas throughout the world. Environmentalists do not want to lose more and more land to highway construction. High-speed trains run on electricity, are nonpolluting, and do not contribute to traffic congestion. In fact, they can relieve congestion because one rail line can be as productive as a ten-lane highway.

With all these advantages in mind, almost every developed nation, including the United States, has been conducting research on new high-speed technology. The theory behind the time, effort, and money spent on this research is that railroads can help solve the world's transportation problems if they can attract more riders. It may seem a waste not to develop the *shinkansen* and TGV further, since that technology is already available. But flanged wheels on rails do not have the potential to do much more. Even with trains that travel less than two hundred miles per hour, there are problems with the special, dedicated tracks. The *shinkansen* track requires almost daily maintenance.

The high-speed trains of the future will be able to go more than three hundred miles per hour and possibly as high as five hundred. Traditional trains simply cannot travel more than three hundred miles per hour on rails because of air resistance and friction between the wheel and rail. Therefore, the next generation of trains is designed to travel without rails. In doing so, it will change the meaning of railroads.

Suspended Between Magnets

The train that will do this is called the maglev, which is short for "magnetic levitation." It was the brainchild of an American scientist named James Powell, who began thinking about it in 1960. His idea was based on the same principle as the Hovercraft, a boat that sails above the surface of the water on a cushion of air. But instead of using air to cushion the train, Powell proposed using magnetism to both support and propel it. The federal government provided three million dollars for research and development of what was called the

Magneplane but then abruptly withdrew funding in 1975. The project died while the *Magneplane* was still only a model. Fortunately, Japan and Germany had already picked up the idea, and by 1979, the Japanese had a maglev that tested at 320 miles per hour. But their project would take another ten years and cost the Japanese government one billion dollars before it was considered ready to go into service. The German maglev has a similar history.

Although the maglev is called a train, it is really more like a very lowflying plane without wings. The theory behind the maglev is that opposite magnetic poles attract each other and like poles repel each other. A typical maglev travels less than an inch above a specially designed guideway. It is suspended between magnets in the guideway and magnets on the bottom of the train. At the same time, the magnets on the bottom of the train are attracted by another

The benefits of high-speed train travel are motivating many nations to invest in new types of train technology.

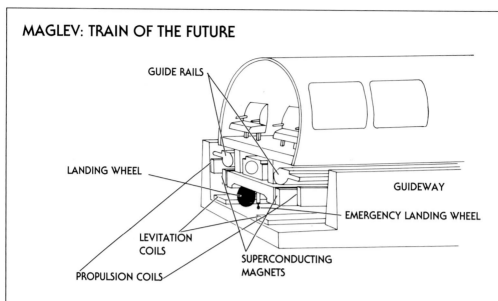

MAGLEV: TRAIN OF THE FUTURE

GUIDE RAILS

LANDING WHEEL

GUIDEWAY

EMERGENCY LANDING WHEEL

LEVITATION COILS

SUPERCONDUCTING MAGNETS

PROPULSION COILS

Magnetic levitation, or maglev, trains like this one are now being tested in many countries. A maglev train contains superconducting magnets that help lift the train above the track and also propel it forward. The train works on the principles of magnetic repulsion and attraction—when two like magnetic poles are side by side, they repel each other, while two opposite poles always attract each other.

The maglev train runs on a special kind of track, called a guideway. Engineers have designed different types of guideways, but the one shown here has two kinds of magnetic coils running through it. One kind of coil called levitation coils runs along the base of the guideway. They have the same magnetic pole as the magnets on the train. The force of these magnets repelling each other lifts the train slightly off the track. The other kind of coils, propulsion coils, are placed on both sides of the guideway and have the opposite pole of the magnets on the train and the levitation coils. As these coils are electronically activated by a computer, they attract the train's superconducting magnets and pull the train forward.

series of special propulsion magnets that are spaced a few feet apart all along the guideway. These propulsion magnets are electrically activated one by one in sequence by computers to pull the train along.

Test Runs

While both the Germans and the Japanese have maglevs running on test tracks, none of them are licensed to carry passengers. The only maglev in the world licensed to carry passengers is a line now being planned for Las Vegas, Nevada. Hoping to develop a world market for its maglev by building a showcase for its technology, the Japanese firm High Speed Surface Transport (HSST) agreed to cover the entire cost of a line through the city. HSST now estimates that its maglev will be traveling at 125 miles per hour on the four-mile line by 1994.

The streamlined HSST maglev resembles the long, sleek body of a very modern, but wingless jetliner. Each train can link any number of cars, and, depending on their size, cars can seat between forty and one hundred passengers. The trains run on an elevated guideway or track. The rails of the guideway are quite different from those built for conventional trains. In place of two parallel steel rails, are two large beams. Rails, made of fairly thin iron, are attached to the top of each beam. In place of wheels, the cars have two U-shaped indentations or slots running along their lower edges. The rails fit into those slots, but the cars do not ride directly on them. Magnets in the rails and slots keep the cars floating a mere three-eighths inch above the rail.

There are many advantages to this innovative new form of rail travel. Because maglevs float, there is no friction to slow them down, no fear of derailment, and less wear and tear on the train and guideway. There also is no vibration, which means passengers enjoy a smooth ride. Furthermore, maglevs are very

(top) A maglev demonstration at a Japanese science exposition carried thousands of passengers.
(bottom) Japanese maglev trains could become the most efficient means of mass transit.

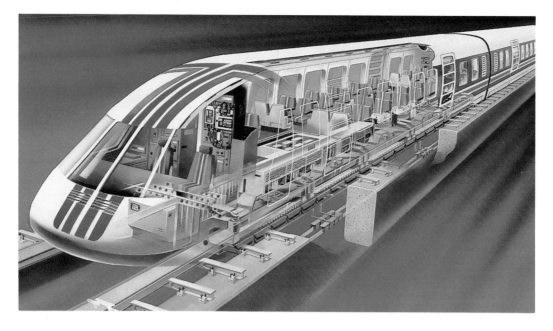

This illustration shows the interior and working parts of a maglev.

quiet, very clean, and use about one-tenth the energy of electric trains. In fact, they have the potential of being the most environmentally sound form of transportation in the world.

Despite these advantages, very few people will be riding a maglev soon. This train of the future took thirty years to develop and is still being modified. One interesting problem being worked on is that the train cannot travel for long periods at high speed. Although maglevs can potentially travel at three hundred to five hundred miles per hour, if they go three hundred miles per hour for more than twenty minutes, they catch on fire. The primary problem, however, is the expense. The estimated cost of the four-mile Las Vegas line is $130 million.

Interest Is High

Oddly enough, it is the United States that seems most interested in high-speed

maglevs. HSST has received at least twenty requests for proposals to build lines in American cities. It has been considered for a transit system in New Jersey, a commuter line in New York, and a people mover between the Orlando, Florida, airport and Disney World. Several million dollars were included in the 1991 federal budget to study maglevs, and a National Maglev Initiative is coordinating developmental efforts by the departments of Transportation and Energy, the Federal Railroad Administration, and private industry. Some senators are actively seeking more money and guarantees for construction loans.

Many experts feel that the *Magneplane* abandoned in 1975 would be cheaper to build and have less technical problems than either the Japanese or German version. Unfortunately, it would take many years to catch up with the technology that is already available.

Maglevs may be the wave of the future for trains, but they will not solve

(top) A maglev is scheduled to begin operation in Las Vegas in 1994.
(bottom) In the future, high-speed trains may play an important role in solving America's transportation problems.

the world's transportation problems the way the steam locomotive did in the early nineteenth century. No single form of transportation can. The world is now far too complex for that. The best solution to transportation problems is a balanced system that includes highways, air routes, and railroads. The emphasis needs to be taken off competition and put on cooperation and coordination. Each kind of transportation should be performing the role it does best: for railroads, that role is to provide economical, environmentally safe mass transport for people and freight.

Glossary

■■

air brake: A brake operated by compressing air in cylinders.

boiler: A large container of heated water that produces steam to run an engine.

brakeman: A railroad worker who set the hand brakes and coupled the cars on trains powered by steam locomotives.

branch line: A secondary rail line off of a main railroad line.

catenary: A wire cable running above a track that supplies electricity to an electric train.

common carrier: A public railroad available to all passengers and freight for a fee.

connecting rod: A rod that connects two train wheels and causes them to turn together.

cowcatcher: A triangular frame on the front of a locomotive designed to clear obstructions off the track as the train moves.

cylinder: A cylindrical chamber in which a piston moves to compress air or a fluid.

dedicated track: A railroad track used only for one type of train, usually a high-speed train.

diesel: An electric locomotive that produces its own power with heat; heated fuel drives a generator that produces electricity.

driving wheels: The wheels rotated by the engine that cause the locomotive to move.

firebox: The container where fuel is burned to heat the water in the boiler of a steam locomotive.

fireman: The railroad worker who fed fuel to the firebox of a steam locomotive.

flanged wheels: Wheels that have rims on the inner edge to keep the train on the track.

knuckle coupler: An automatic device that links cars of a train together.

leading truck: A separate, swiveled undercarriage beneath the front end of a steam locomotive; helps locomotives maintain stability on uneven tracks and go smoothly around curves.

maglev: A train that operates by magnetic levitation.

pantograph: A hinged device that conducts electricity from an overhead wire to an electric locomotive.

piston: A disk or cylindrical device that fits tightly into a cylinder and moves back and forth to compress air or a fluid.

plated rail: A wooden rail with a strip of iron nailed on top of it.

rate discrimination: Charging some customers higher rates than others for the same service or product.

rebate: A partial refund of a payment already made for a service or product.

rolling stock: All the cars and locomotives of a railroad.

shoe: A device on an electric locomotive that picks up electricity from a third rail.

smoke box: A container on a steam locomotive that traps the smoke, sparks, and excess steam, which then escape out of the smokestack.

smokestack: A funnel on a steam locomotive that lets the smoke, sparks, and excess steam escape into the air.

steam dome: The container on a steam locomotive where the steam goes after leaving the boiler.

stock: A certificate that represents part ownership of a company.

streamliner: A train with modern, sleek lines.

tender: A fuel-carrying car pulled just behind a steam locomotive.

third rail: A rail beside the track that conducts electricity to power an electric locomotive.

For Further Reading

Lucius Beebe, *Mansions on Rails: The Folklore of the Private Railway Car.* Berkeley, CA: Howell-North Press, 1959.

Ray Broekel, *Trains.* Chicago: Children's Press, 1981.

Rixon Bucknall, *Trains.* New York: Grosset & Dunlap, 1973.

Paul C. Ditzel, *Railroad Yard.* New York: Julian Messner, 1977.

Frank P. Donovan, Jr., and Robert Selph Henry, eds. *Headlights and Markers: An Anthology of Railroad Stories.* New York: Creative Age Press, 1946.

George Dow, *World Locomotive Models.* New York: Arco Publishing, 1973.

John Everds, *The Spectacular Trains: A History of Rail Transportation.* Northbrook, IL: Hubbard Press, 1973.

Dennis R. Flatley, *Opening the West: The Railroads.* New York: Franklin Watts, 1989.

Brian Haresnape, *Everyone's Color Book of Trains.* New York: Hamlyn, 1981.

Stewart H. Holbrook, *The Golden Age of Railroads.* New York: Random House, 1960.

Freeman H. Hubbard, *Railroad Avenue: Great Stories and Legends of American Railroading.* New York: McGraw-Hill, 1945.

Samuel Moskowitz, ed. *Great Railroad Stories of the World.* New York: McBride, 1954.

John Gabriel Navarra, *Supertrains.* Garden City, NY: Doubleday, 1976.

Richard Patterson, *Train Robbery: The Birth, Flowering, and Decline of a Notorious Western Enterprise.* Boulder, CO: Johnson Books, 1981.

Walter Retan, *The Big Book of Real Trains.* New York: Grosset & Dunlap, 1987.

Paul I. Wellman, *Race to the Golden Spike.* Boston: Houghton Mifflin, 1961.

Keith Wheeler, *The Railroaders.* New York: Time-Life Books, 1973.

Works Consulted

G. Freeman Allen, *Railways: Past, Present & Future*. New York: William Morrow, 1982.

Keith L. Bryant, Jr., ed. "Railroads in the Age of Regulation, 1900–1980," *Encyclopedia of American Business History & Biography*. New York: Facts on File Publications, 1988.

Reginald Carpenter, Peter Kalla-Bishop, Kenneth Munson, and Robert Wyatt, *Powered Vehicles: A Historical Review*. New York: Crown, 1974.

George H. Drury, *The Historical Guide to North American Railroads*. Milwaukee: Kalmbach Publishing, 1985.

C. Hamilton Ellis, *Railway History*. New York: Dutton, 1966.

John A. Francis, *A History of the English Railway: Its Social Relations & Revelations, 1820–1845*. London: Longman, Brown, Green & Longmans, 1851. Reprint. New York: Augustus M. Kelley, 1968.

Rolt Hammond, *Railways in the New Air Age*. London: Oxford University Press, 1964.

Aaron E. Klein, *Supertrains*. New York: Exeter Books, 1985.

O.S. Nock, *The Dawn of World Railways, 1800–1850*. London: Blandford Press, 1972.

Paul North, *American Steam Locomotives*. New York: Gallery Books, 1988.

Jefferey Richards and John M. MacKenzie. *The Railway Station: A Social History*. Oxford: Oxford University Press, 1986.

Anthony Ridley, *An Illustrated History of Transportation*. New York: John Day, 1969.

Roy V. Scott, *Railroad Development Programs in the Twentieth Century*. Ames: Iowa State University Press, 1985.

John R. Stilgoe, *Metropolitan Corridor: Railroads and the American Scene*. New Haven: Yale University Press, 1983.

Edward L. Throm, ed. *Popular Mechanics' Picture History of American Transportation*. New York: Simon & Schuster, 1952.

James A. Ward, *Railroads and the Character of America, 1820–1887*. Knoxville: The University of Tennessee Press, 1986.

George Zaffo, *Airplanes and Trucks and Trains, Fire Engines, Boats and Ships and Building and Wrecking Machines*. New York: Grosset & Dunlap, 1979.

Index

About the Author

Lois Warburton earned her master's degree in education at Clark University in Worcester, Massachusetts. Her previous published works include nonfiction articles, magazine columns, short stories, and poetry. In 1990, she retired from her own word processing, writing, and editing business to travel and write books. This is her fourth book for Lucent Books.

Picture Credits